MW01153853

prologue

When I initially started working on this project, I had a smile painted across my face. The aes-
thetic was completed with witty comments and com-
pelling stories about how great my life was, and how
exhilarating and adventurous my days had become. I
was as hidden as I had ever been, both from myself
and from the world. I thought I knew all the answers.
I thought I had gone through my healing, sat through
enough therapy sessions, read enough self-help
books, and was prepared to move onto the other side
with gold stars and wisdom to show.

I am not generally the most patient person,
which I've been learning the hard way about myself
through the process of writing this book. Oh, I had
plenty of advice to share with you about what it
means to belong, while conversely, still having no
idea what it meant myself. After a full year of working day and night to complete that version of this
story, I am finding myself in "belonging" for the first

time in my life, and realizing I need to start again from the beginning. So, many hours and drafts and edits later, here we are, back at the prologue. But the work has been good, and each draft has peeled back even more layers of healing, self-discovery, and answers to questions I was too afraid to ask before. I am proud of the story you're holding in your hands.

This story seemingly starts with an impulsive move to a city I barely knew. It looks like the beginning of a grand, spontaneous adventure of learning to make a home in a city I hadn't spent longer than 48 hours in. But in more honest language, it's a sacred story that's been writing itself over the two and near-half decades since I was born. It's a beginning and a middle and an end all wrapped into one. But for now, we'll start with this: On a three-day notice at the end of a two-month summer tour, I packed up my life and moved to Boston.

Sitting side by side on the trendy metal stools inside the only decent coffee shop we could find in the middle of Las Vegas, my best friend, Kate, tapped me on the shoulder.

"Jackie, I have something to ask you."

I gazed down at the freshly poured cappuccino waiting to be enjoyed on the table in front of me and held my breath as I waited for a question that would change the course of my life.

"Okay," I responded hesitantly, shifting myself to face her. She looked nervous, anxious almost as if she had been biting her tongue wanting to ask me this all summer.

"Jackie, I want to offer you a job to be my full-time assistant. But the thing is, you'd have to move to Boston. I want you to come back to Boston with me after tour, like, as soon as possible."

"Wait," I stuttered, "are you serious?"

My chest tightened as I tried to find the right words to respond to a question like this. My whole summer had been spent selling T-shirts with her name on it, listening to her band's set on repeat, and waking up before anyone else on the tour bus to make coffee and toast so she could have breakfast waiting when she woke up. And though my whole world was required to revolve around someone else, it was a welcome distraction from myself. I found life on tour refreshingly simple, and I was scared to leave it and reenter a chaotic, "normal" life with all my familiar personal baggage in three short days when our summer tour would end.

I have moved thirteen times since leaving my childhood home at nineteen. I am now twenty-four. Last year I moved eight times alone, which was what led me to consider: What have I been chasing? What does home mean? It was that wondering that wooed me into writing this book.

As a child, I was a happy-go-lucky little girl spinning around in a light pink nightgown, begging and pleading for her big sister to let her play too. I'd run downstairs to the basement while her friends were over, each performing dances to the Annie soundtrack in front of my dad's video camera. I'd fall to my knees and beg to play too, but rarely got the invite.

It was hard for me to feel good enough in most areas in my family. My brains and talents were constantly being compared to my big sister who from the outside looking in, could do no wrong. I was literally told by family members to "hold onto my sister's coattails" in life. After talking about my own career dreams, hearing words like, "Well, you know what? I think you should just start a worldwide fan club for your sister!" That mixed with nicknames like, "putz" or "moron," when I threw the ball too much "like a girl", made it clear that I wasn't quite what was expected. By the time I turned 17, I was tired of trying to squeeze into someone else's shoes and started saving to move out of my parent's house and start over elsewhere. Someplace where I could forge my own path into my future without being in the shadow of other people's judgments and expectations.

At 19, I moved to Los Angeles to fulfill my childhood dreams of becoming a dolphin trainer. But plans changed pretty quickly. When I arrived, I immediately landed what I thought was a dream job. I worked for a year as a personal assistant to a semi-successful musician. As it happened, "assisting" turned out to be a euphemism for "parenting a 31-year-old man." My boss was a narcissistic, emotionally-abusive musician who lied about his age. My job involved driving him around, making his breakfast, and doing his laundry. He quite literally asked me to smell his dirty socks and underwear to see if they needed to be washed. (He, of course, could not find the time to separate the proverbial sheep from the goats himself--after all, there were so many pop songs that needed to be covered!)

Our story of origin was questionable as well. I was connected to the job because he dated (and emotionally abused) my sister for about two years. Once they finally broke up, he (my boss) would get wasted and put the moves on me regardless of how I felt. The first encounter was a drunken kiss while we were on tour, two days after my sister called things off with him. He took me to a bar, sat in the booth and put his head down on the table. I tried to see if he was okay, when my 31-year-old boss, out of nowhere, sat up and grabbed my head to kiss me. After it happened, I curled up outside the tour bus with a blanket and cried myself to sleep in the parking lot. It was a devastating interpersonal dynamic, and devastatingly continued this way for too long.

There were many more "drunken mistakes" after that, some of which were mine, before we both "found Jesus together." At the end of my two years in LA, I had simultaneously been in a highly toxic, secretive, and exploitative relationship with my sister's ex-boyfriend, and had jumped head first into the evangelical church culture partially in an effort to circumvent the discomfort and shame in my spirit. Unfortunately, involvement in a trendy church was not enough on its own to keep me together. Shortly thereafter, my life hit a very rocky rock bottom.

As I started to come clean and open up about my shame story for the first time ever, letting people know what happened with my boss and the abuse I endured working for him, my church-based community in LA proved itself unsafe. Condemning letters listing my failures and character flaws were written and read aloud to me. I was banished from our community group for "not being honest about what had happened with the man." Some of my closest friends at the time, ones who had claimed to be in my corner, suddenly started a band with the dude the same night everything started to fall apart. They no longer spoke to me after that. (Of course, the 31-year-old man was allowed to stay in the community group and move forward safely through the fallout because, as I was told, "he really needed his friends through this hard time.")

Needless to say, I was done feeling at home in Los Angeles and found myself ready to move on to something new.

At age 21, I packed up my life and moved to Nashville. As an escape from the chaos of LA, I ran away to a ministry school in an attempt to find purpose and belonging there instead. I didn't grow up in the church world, and the ones I went to in LA were fairly "normal." However, the ministry school I found was a bit out of my comfort zone. Imagine the culture shock going from that to an environment where a giant exorcism was a regular part of the school day. In one particular theatrical episode, fifty of my friends rolled around on the ground as if they were having cluster seizures. I cried in the corner while they made animal sounds and thrashed about until my school pastor approached me, asking, "What's wrong with you? What trauma from your past is this triggering?" *This is the trauma, lady,* I thought, resolving at that moment to drop out of the school and find a new way forward. But in that leaving, the church became an identity crisis of its own.

Beyond that, I had a hard time finding my place among friends as well. During the one year I lived in Nashville, I moved three times and broke two leases. I shuffled around for many reasons and was met with odd replies and strange takes at every turn. From, "God told me you were moving out," to, "God told me I'm supposed to have the bigger room," to being yelled at on almost a nightly basis about my character being broken, my compliments being fake. I was also chastised for hugging men, since "they might remember that touch and be unfaithful to their wife someday." That, on top of your classic relation-ship drama, church problems, and Christian leader-ship done terribly wrong, left me wanting to run away from Nashville as well.

So, there I was sitting next to my best friend at the end of our summer tour. Now 23 years old, whiplashed from the various moments of running away disguised as moving, the toxic relationships and baggage after baggage of shame, just wanting to know where I belonged. Memories of my nomadic lifestyle, all the moves I had made, all the dreams of belonging and sanctuary that I couldn't quite reach filled my mind. If I said yes to this new adventure, this had to be it for me. It had to work. I believed, at that moment, that everything had pointed me here, and saying no to the opportunity didn't feel like an option. If I agreed, there would be no going back. If I said yes, I needed it to be my final stop. *And if I go,* I thought, *I think I could finally, maybe, really be home.*

"Yes," I answered. "I'll move to Boston. I'm in."

PART ONE

adrift

escape

With four giant bags dragging along behind me, I forced my legs to quicken their pace as I started to make my way inside the Boston airport. It had been barely three months since I said yes to this grand adventure. Three months since I stepped off the red-eye flight after tour into this new city with my best friend by my side, and now I was instantaneously on my way out, alone.

"Have a nice trip!" the Lyft driver shouted through the window before driving off. I heard him loud and clear, yet no part of me felt capable of playing my part in his attempted cheerful conversation.

After making it inside, I instantly became aware of how many people found it amusing to make fun of me for "traveling so light" as I fumbled through the airport terminals on my way out of Boston. I can't say I blamed them. I was in the middle of yet another move and literally traveling with everything I owned. However, not one little bit of me could play along with their witty remarks.

"This isn't a weekend trip, this is everything I own!" I snapped, unable to remain in composure. I didn't expect to be making this move today. It had been only three months since I said yes and impulsively moved my life to Boston to work for my best friend, and less than three hours ago I was instructed to leave. Feeling defeated, I pulled my bags up to the front desk and threw them on the scale.

"Hello there, young lady. Can I get your license and address please?" The clerk asked.

Are you kidding me? I've had more addresses in the past two years than I'd had in the 20 before that. This past year alone I had moved eight times. What was I supposed to tell her? It's not a fair question to be asked in the middle of a nomadic crisis. Standing in this airport with a line of impatient travelers waiting behind me, I had never been more painfully aware of my lack of a home.

After finally working through the extensive list of zip codes with the lady, I was handed my ticket and on my way. The hallways felt cold, bitter, isolating. My body didn't feel like it was a part of me anymore, as if my soul was floating around in the sky watching my defected person shuffle through the airport.

My surroundings grew blurry, my eyes saw everything move half a second behind. Who am I? How did I get here? I thought to myself as I stood still waiting to go through security. In the line with me, I watched the couples holding hands, the mothers holding their daughters, and the fathers smiling in their presence. They belonged together. I saw best friends laughing side by side, snuggled up tightly in their matching winter coats. Not me. I was alone, and I felt as if the whole world knew.

I got through security and realized that it was time to start moving again. I stared at the ground as I hurtled through the terminal, ashamed of showing my face to the travelers walking past me.

I decided to take a quick detour into the bathroom to wash my hands, as if somehow doing so would remove a layer of shame I had stuck to my body. There, standing in front of the sink, I lifted my stare from my soapy hands to the reflection in the mirror. Suddenly, I was face to face with myself. I hated myself. I hated my face, my body, my hands. I saw brokenness in my skin, pain, and failure in my eyes. There was no life in them, nor was there power or courage, but I couldn't look away. I felt like a bad car accident, the kind other drivers slow down to see the damage.

I left the bathroom and sat down on the floor to wait by my gate.

"Flight 605 to Nashville will be boarding in twenty minutes," I heard over the loud intercoms. That was too long, I needed to leave now. I couldn't sit in this state for one moment longer. I couldn't stand the thought of being in Boston for one more second. I wasn't welcome here anymore. I felt like an exile, a homeless nobody that people wanted to get away from. I was a failure here.

I found myself surrounded by other travelers enjoying their dinners. Sandwiches, pizza, pasta, burritos, no food group got left behind in this airport. It all looked so good. I was starving, so much so that I had forgotten what it felt like to be full. My body didn't deserve food right now. Food gave life, and I wasn't worthy of that.

Staring down at the ground, my body grew numb. The voices around me faded off into the air, and I felt unable to stay present. Everything I knew to be true about myself, everyone I thought I had trusted, it had all vanished. Was this my fault? Am I this despicable of a human being that I deserved to be banished from a whole city? I must be, there's no other explanation that I could make sense out of in my tired mind. I closed my eyes and pretended I was invisible.

Right there sitting at my gate in the Boston airport, I wished I was dead. I had longed for that with so much of my heart over the past three months, but it had yet to feel this urgent. Those thoughts used to terrify me, laying alone in the various hotel beds that didn't belong to me. But not anymore. There in the airport, the thought of staying alive felt more terrifying than the thought of dying.

The quietness grew too loud. I instinctively reached for my phone to text my best friend, Kate, then quickly put it back down on the floor. Texting her wasn't allowed anymore, I remembered. I was ordered not to do that. I pulled out my Jane Austen book from my backpack instead, flipping to the page I left off on.

"Why," I whispered, "why am I still reading this book?"

Because I recalled, everyone else in Boston was. I had to fit in, I had to have knowledge about these pieces of literature that everyone else had whether I had real interest or not. I couldn't let them know I wasn't as smart as them. I couldn't let them know I wasn't as interesting.

But here in this airport, why? I no longer have a reason to hide. My attempt to belong had already failed. I was already exposed, exiled, and alone. I wasn't fooling myself, so what's the point? I stood up, walked to put the Jane Austen book on a faraway table, and sat back down in my seat. Maybe somebody else, somewhere in the middle of their journey, will find more joy from Pride and Prejudice than me right now.

I had never been less sure about who I was. I had never wanted out of my own body as desperately as I did then.

The brutally long twenty minutes finally came to an end. I got myself up and boarded my flight. I was headed for Nashville, but at this point in time anywhere else in the world would do. Just take me away from here.

Eyes closed, heartbroken, power diminished, I leaned back into my seat and breathed in my last bit of Boston air. For now, I was safe.

I

I'm 18 years old. I look out the window inside my mom's car as the mountains start to grow bigger--we are moving, by the minute, closer to my new home. The window is smudged from my heavy breathing, and I draw smiley faces in the fog. My nerves surge. There's no going back now.

College never felt like a chapter that would hold a place in my story; I've never felt quite like I would belong in such a place. I've always dreamt of living by the ocean, training dolphins, and riding my longboard up the PCH on my way to work. But here I am, on my way to my University, with no idea what this next year will hold.

"Jackie, we're almost there. Are you excited?" my mom asks with a hopeful smile as we get off the last exit.

"Yeah. I mean, kind of. I just wish I knew people here. I wish I had friends waiting for me," I answer half-honestly, as I am much more scared than I am willing to admit.

"I know, sweetie, but you'll make friends in no time."

I sigh, swallow my anxiety, and lean my head back up against the window for the remainder of the drive.

We pull up front, park in the closest spot we can find, and begin to unpack all the pink from the trunk--pink lamps, pink posters, pink bed sheets, pink chairs. With boxes in hands, we explore campus until we find my dorm, where we empty our arms of all my cotton-candy belongings and begin finding places for them in the room where I now live.

"Okay, Jackie, we're going to leave now. Are you okay? Is there anything else you need?" my mom asks as we finally finish turning the contents of the car into the contents of my room.

"No. I'm okay. I can do this."

I follow my family downstairs, soaking in every second I can before I am alone again.

"We love you, we'll talk soon!" they shout from the window then drive off. I stay and watch them shrink smaller and smaller as they go until they vanish altogether. This is my life now. I am alone.

The sun starts to set, and I make my way back into my room. I sit beside my lofted bed, concealing all feelings of isolation to the far back corners of my mind. With too many boxes to unpack and too much silence for my liking, I open my computer. A distraction from the alone.

What am I in for here? Who will I meet, and will they even like me? I hug my knees tight to my chest and let myself cry. One positive, I suppose, of being completely alone. I lift my head from my tear-stained knees and look at the empty walls, empty drawers, empty bookshelves, and untouched bed. This is my life now. I will find my purpose here, somehow. I get up, put my shoes on, and walk out the door.

A week goes by, and not a lot of sleep or studying is yet involved in my new college experience. I find a couple of girls to fill the role of temporary best friends and have made a name for myself by finishing my own bottle of vodka every night. My new friends and I parade across campus arm-in-arm, chins up and ready to party.

"Jax! We just scored an invite to the hot guys' dorm. You down? They've got beer pong already set up and I think that one guy who's been checking you out is gonna be there."

"Yeah, obviously I'm down, let me just finish this drink really quick," I answer as I chug the rest of my homemade straight vodka cocktail. I stand with a waver, trip over the Kings Cup game we're playing, stumble into the bathroom to check my makeup, and follow them out the door.

"Hey! There you girls are. We've been waiting for the party to arrive!" the guys in the dorm shout sloppily as we walk through the door. Empty red solo cups and beer bottles are spread out around the floor, and the whole room reeks of weed. But we don't seem to care as we flip our hair back and let ourselves be admired by the hot drunk guys staring us up and down.

"Let's take a shot, quick!" My friend whispers in my ear as she pulls me into the kitchen towards a half drank bottle of liquor sitting on the counter, "I think your man is almost here."

Stumbling over the empty bottles that continued to trail into the kitchen, I put back the shot and smile. We walk back over to the living room where the guys were waiting for us to start beer pong. There he is, my guy, waiting for me on the couch.

"Go sit down with him, Jackie! We'll be over here."

I adjust my way-too-high-waisted shorts and wipe the vodka remnants from my chin as I go to sit beside him.

"Hey beautiful," he says staring down to my chest, "how's your night?"

Before I can respond, his hand grabs the back of my head and pulls me in towards himself. His mouth tastes like cigarettes and beer, but I close my eyes and pretend to enjoy it. At this moment, I don't matter. Only he does.

About ten minutes go by and he seems to have had enough of me. He stands up from the couch to get another beer from the kitchen. I stay and sit by myself, grab my phone and pretend not to care.

The party slowly comes to an end. As the last guy in the dorm falls onto his bed to go to sleep, my friends and I begin to make our way back to our rooms as well. Too drunk to have an actual conversation, we stumble in silence.

Back in my dorm, I crawl into bed fully clothed with leftover makeup smudged underneath my eyes. I pull the blankets over my face and burst into tears. My head is pounding and I can't sleep, so I shift myself around and continue to cry. Hours slowly pass by. I am exhausted, but my mind won't shut off. I look out the window and see the sun begin to rise. The rest of the world is probably waking up, starting their days of work or class. Not me. I don't belong to that world. I stay in bed and continue to cry.

I'm alone. Nobody knows me. Nobody wants to know me. I wish I didn't exist.

———

"Jackie, we're almost here," Kate whispered in my ear as our plane began to descend into Boston. It had been three days since she invited me on this adventure, and I had yet to catch my breath. Slowly peeling my eyes open from the barely two-hour night's sleep I had on our flight after the last night of tour, I looked out the window and saw my new home. There was Boston; my new adventure awaits.

I quickly collected the eclectic books that fell out of my bag during the flight, slipped my shoes back on my feet and took a deep breath in. I can do this.

After landing and gathering our bags, we were quickly hugged goodbye by Kate's parents and got in the car that would take us into Boston. I sat so still in this car, eyes glued to the window, too tired to process what was happening.

"Are you okay, Jackie?" My best friend, now boss, asked.

"Yes," I looked over to answer with a tired smile, "I'm just taking it all in."

We pulled up to a coffee shop called Tatte, which might as well had been a set for all Instagram bloggers to take photos in front of. This place was polished and perfect and much too expensive for its own good. We ordered our coffees, and I waited by the sugars while my friend sought out a place for us to sit down.

"Over here!" Kate shouted as she waved me over to a tiny table by the window.

I picked up my coffee and ventured through the crowds of students getting in their last minutes of studying before class and sat facing my friend. We stared blankly at each other, not sure of what words to use to express how we felt in this moment. Neither one of us knew the depths of what we were in for, yet we were both highly aware of the newness at hand.

"The driver will take you to your hotel and when I'm done with my class, he'll pick you up again to come help me set up my dorm. Is that okay?"

"Yeah, that sounds great," I said forcing my mouth into a smile.

"I'm really excited for this, Jackie. You're like the Sam to my Frodo. Do you know what that means?"

"No, I've never seen Lord of the Rings."

"I'll put it this way: you're my sister, Jackie. You're part of my mission, my family. You're helping me so much more than you know."

I smiled, gushing at the idea of being a part of something that seemed so special and dignified. We hugged goodbye, she walked across the street to her class, and I got in the car waiting to take me to my hotel. I returned to the silence of my own mind as I sat in the car and re-glued my eyes to the window. The buildings looked so welcoming, cluttered with bricks and rustic fire escapes. Green vines wrapped tightly around the poles, the leaves on the trees just recently began to exchange their green wardrobes for red and orange. There's no going back now. I've got this. I will find my purpose here.

We pulled up in front of the hotel. I said goodbye to my driver and pulled my suitcases inside. A lobby full of strangers turned to look as I rolled my loud red bag onto a luggage cart and asked for my room key.

Upstairs in my room, a fluffy white freshly made bed was waiting. I threw my bags in the corner, traded my jeans for sweat pants, and curled up inside the covers. I was physically and emotionally exhausted. I hadn't slept in a bed outside of a cramped bunk on a tour bus in what felt like ages. I closed my eyes, breathed in three deep breaths, and imagined what laid ahead of me here. What would this city add to my story? Where would I find my belonging? I knew nobody, nobody knew me, and I hadn't the slightest clue how to ride a subway.

The walls looked empty. Not literally, as they did have the classic hotel approved photos of flowers and trees. But none of the photos belonged to me. I looked over at the desk by the window to notice a stack of books, none of which were mine either. I turned over on my side and gazed out the window at the river instead. "I'm going to be okay," I whispered to myself as I closed my eyes to rest.

A week or so into my time there, I was invited to dinner with my best friend and her classmates. I grabbed my favorite jacket, checked my hair one last time in the hotel mirror, and walked out to meet Kate and her friends in the dorms.

"Jackie! We're over here!" I heard as I walked up the steps.

"Hey, how was your day? How was class?"

"Great! We were learning about (insert some very smart philosophical language here that I didn't understand)." I nodded along as if I knew exactly what they were talking about.

We arrived at the restaurant, and food I've never heard of was quickly ordered and set down in the middle to share. They talked amongst themselves; I twiddled my thumbs underneath the table without knowing what was interesting that I could add to the conversation. I nodded, laughed when it seemed appropriate, and asked questions to keep the conversation going when I noticed a lag.

The dinner came to an end, we said our goodbyes, they walked to their dorms and I headed back to my hotel. Slowly pushing the door open, I tripped walking through the dark room and slid back into bed. I rolled onto my side to stare at the city lights out the window. What just happened? I thought to myself. Did I do okay? Did they like me? Did I ask good enough questions? I was all alone now and finally allowed to be honest with myself and cry. This was my fresh start. This was my new life. This was my new home. But where is my place here?

I'm alone. Nobody knows me. Nobody wants to know me. I wish I didn't exist.

II

I'm 19 years old, living on a tour bus for the first time in my life. Adventure and travel have always been a deep love of mine, so I have high hopes for what this experience will have in store. I left college after the first semester and moved to LA with the intention of training dolphins, but my sister's boyfriend offered me a job to be his personal assistant instead. Without thinking twice, I said yes. I never thought I'd have an opportunity like this. I always thought these kinds of adventures were for other people, not me. Who am I to get to travel around with a rock band all summer?

My hair is bleached blonde partially because I'm obsessed with the character Rachel Green from the show Friends, and partially because I think it makes me attractive. I also get compared to my sister Alex all the time, and I just want to look like my own person right now. I don't know, I'm figuring it out, I guess. My wardrobe consists of high waisted short-shorts with holes on the hips, cowboy boots, and white lace tank tops. I wear a lot of makeup to hide whatever is naturally unappealing on my face, but I hope people don't notice.

Living on the road feels so magnificent on tour, like nothing else exists. I've never felt more special and a part of something. I've never felt so important. When I was offered this job to be a personal assistant to a professional musician, nothing else in the world made sense. Maybe this is what I'm supposed to do, maybe this career is where I'll find my purpose and belonging.

"JAX! Do you have your fake ID on you? We're going to a bar before the show, come on!" my boss, Steve, yells across the bus. My sister told him not to drink around me since I had a bad history with it before moving to LA. I used to party too much and end up in really terrible situations, using drinking and parties to numb out when life felt too painful to be present for. But Steve doesn't seem to be listening to her, so I guess I won't either.

"Yeah, got it! Let's go!"

A few days go by. I find out my sister and him break up. I don't really know what it means for them or for me, but everyone seems to be okay. I carry on with my job and wait for a call from Alex that doesn't come.

34

The show ends and we all head back to the green room to take more shots before the meet and greets start. Some of the "guests" pay to meet the boss. My job is to point them out and give him the information he needs to make intelligent conversation and ensure that they feel they got their money's worth. It's not too unlike my job with him at parties, following him around taking notes on my phone of all the people he meets so that he'll remember. Not all of them, just the important ones that can offer him something he wants to further his career.

The meet and greets are done now and my boss's friends offer to take him and I to get some food across the street. They're in the front seat, Steve and I are in the back. He's acting really weird and flirty, as never before, which is extremely confusing. He's an important guy. I'm not sure why he has interest in me all of a sudden, but I'm probably reading it wrong.

Suddenly, he leans over on my side of the car and puts his arms around my waist, grabbing my hand as if it was supposed to belong to him. I don't say anything.

His friends drop us back off at the tour bus, and he asks me to go talk with him in the back room.

I do as I'm told. I sit down on the floor, he locks the door.

"Jackie, have you ever, like, I don't know, thought about you and me? Like, together?" he asks with a childish grin on his face.

I don't know what to say or how to respond. No, I never had. He's 31, I'm 19, and he dated my sister and was now my boss. Also, what would an important guy like him want with a young, naive teenager like me?

"No, why?" I respond. We are interrupted by another member of the band trying to get into the room we're locked in. My boss changes the subject and acts like nothing happened.

The next morning, I lay there in my bunk anxious and confused, unsure if I did something wrong. *Did I initiate something? Did I make it seem like I was interested in him without realizing?* I crawl out of my bunk and start to walk over to the bathroom as his hand pops out from behind his curtain to grab my arm.

"Hey, let's pretend last night didn't happen. I shouldn't have said anything." I agree, laugh to kill the awkwardness, and carry on with my morning.

Later that night we prepare for another show. Shots are being taken, I'm stumbling over a load of Steve's laundry I'm supposed to get done before setting up merch. Time is ticking, and I'm three shots behind everyone else. I feel a little sick, but I have to catch up.

A few hours later, the show and meet and greets end. Steve stumbles out of the venue not wanting to sign any more T-shirts, then invites a few of the fans onto our bus to hang out. We all sit down awkwardly on the couch. None of the band members seem to be in the mood to entertain the random teenage girls my boss imposed on them.

Next thing I know, Steve grabs my hand and pulls me off the bus to jump into an Uber that takes us to a bar. Sitting in the booth, he puts his head down into his arms. I shake him to wake up, wondering if he's okay.

His head finally lifts up off the table and within two seconds, his hand grabs my head and his lips are pushed onto mine. *What is happening?*

I run to the bathroom to collect myself, unsure how to handle the wave of emotions that have now taken over my entire body. Staring at myself in the mirror, I wonder who I have become. I start to hate myself.

I walk out to see if he's still there in the booth. He sees me and pulls me outside to sit on the ground beside the bar, trying to recollect what just happened. He leans in again to kiss me, this time his hand grazing up my inner thigh. I hate myself, and I don't know how to stop what's happening. I say nothing. I just sit there and let him do whatever he wants. He's in charge, my power belongs to him.

We look up and see our tour bus driving by across the street. He grabs my hand and pulls me to chase it down.

"Wait!" he yells. I follow behind. Our driver stops and lets us in. We walk in and sit down on the couch as if nothing happened. The rest of the band seems confused, but my boss is acting normal. I guess I'll act normal too.

Our bus pulls over into a hotel parking lot to let the driver take a break, and everyone else is still hanging out up front. An overwhelming self-hatred enters my body, my soul, my whole being. I have never felt this before. I don't know where to go from here, so I run to my bunk and grab my blanket as if I was a little girl again.

After pulling my blanket off my bed, I go outside the tour bus and curl up in a ball leaned up against the tire. I am ashamed, scared, disgusted with who I had become.

Morning is here. I can't exactly remember how I stumbled back onto the bus the night before, but everyone keeps making fun of me for almost being left behind. We're in a new city that I don't know the name of, but I just want to lay here in my bunk for a while longer. I wish I could die today. I stare at the ceiling and feel trapped. There's not one thing that can get me out of this now. I hate myself. I am disgusting, evil, despicable. Who do I think I am? There's not a single human being on the face of the earth who is as terrible as me. I deserve death. I feel around my breast as if I *hopefully* think I'll find a lump. I deserve cancer, I deserve any disease that can take away my life right now. There's no getting out of this, the burn in my chest feels too hot to not be real. I wish I was dead.

"Jackie! You have to get up, we're all going to this amusement park and you're about to be left behind again!" A voice says from the other side of the curtain. Slapping myself in the face, I slip out of my bunk and pretend not to have a hangover. After a quick glance in the bathroom mirror to check my hair, I head out the door.

"Hey, so, about last night," Steve says the second he gets me alone, "we can just agree to pretend that that didn't happen, right? I mean that shouldn't have happened."

"Yeah, okay," I respond, pretending not to care.

This pattern of get-drunk-make-out-then-pretend-nothing-happened continues for the rest of the tour. After the last show, we head to LA for an event called Vidcon. My sister texts me, asking me to come see her get baptized the day we arrive. I don't make arrangements to do so because I'm too ashamed to see her face.

At Vidcon, Steve is the most drunk I've ever seen him. He grabs my hand as we climb up the escalator. I wish I can say I don't like it, but he makes me feel important. We're headed to a party now, one that only the top YouTubers got invited to. He leaves me for a while, so I hang out by the snack table picking at shrimp and chips to pass the time. I'm not sure what else to do when I see a security guard grabbing my boss by his shirt and pulling him out of the party.

Am I supposed to go with him? I wonder. I'm his assistant, and honestly, I'm not enjoying the party anyway, so I follow him out.

We're now in the hotel lobby. I'm yelling at him for getting that drunk and he's pretending not to care. I follow him into the hotel room we were sharing with our friends and continue to yell as he says nothing. The lights are off, I'm standing in front of him, he pushes me down on top of the bed and crawls on top of me. He kisses me, and again I don't stop him. I instantly hate myself even more.

We're interrupted by our friend trying to get into the room. I frantically put my shirt back on that he took off and jump into my rollaway bed to hide under the covers.

Hours pass, everyone is back and in bed now. I can't sleep. I see a bottle of Sailor Jerry's rum next to my bed, pick it up, and consider finishing it off. I want to escape.

I have never despised myself this much. Who am I? Why am I doing this to myself? To my sister? I'm so lost and confused and I don't know who I am, but I can't lose this job because it gives me the only identity I have. Being his assistant gives me purpose, but it's destroying my soul. I want to kill myself, I so badly do. I hate my boss. I hate myself. I want to die.

———

I woke up early one morning to a text from my best friend, now boss, asking me to make her breakfast and bring it to her dorm before her class.

"Yeah, I'll get up and make it right now and be there soon!" I text back.

It was freezing outside, as Boston generally is that time of year. I bundled up in my jacket and scarves after preparing Kate's breakfast, hopped on my bike to ride across town to her dorm.

I pulled up to her building, locked up my bike with the intention of going inside to hang out for a bit. It's been so lonely here lately, I wasn't really sure how to escape it. There was an honest part of me that was thankful to ride my bike early in the morning in the cold if it meant avoiding the isolation of my Airbnb.

I didn't have a key to get in, so I texted Kate to let her know that I was waiting outside. It was so cold, my toes started to go numb. About ten minutes later, she finally responded and was heading down to pick up her breakfast.

"Oh, thank you," Kate said as she reached for the almond butter toast I had made her. "I have studying to do, so I'll see you later!"

"Oh, okay! Yeah, of course. No problem. Have a great day at school, let me know if there's anything else you need later," I said, trying as hard as I could to not let her know I had assumed she was going to invite me in.

I rode my bike from her dorm to Tatte, the coffee shop that I spent the majority of my time in. I walked in, situated myself in my favorite booth by the window, and opened up my book to read for a little while. My job duties were still being worked out, so for now, that meant being on-call at all times. That being said, I never wanted to go off too far. I never knew if my boss would need me for something, even if it was just going to get her breakfast or coffee. This job was what gave me any sort of purpose in Boston. The thought of doing something wrong, of not being available when needed, was unacceptable.

About a week later, we headed to New York City for an event Kate was asked to perform at. A private driver dropped us off at the train station, which made me feel way more important than I actually was.

After the train ride came to an end, we got in another car that would take us to our hotel. We were staying in one of the most esteemed hotels in New York, which again made me feel like I was a part of something much more prominent than I deserved to be. We walked into the lobby and were instantly greeted by the bellhop who took our bags and handed us our keys. We walked upstairs and into our room where our bags had already arrived.

"Do you want to order room service, Jackie?"

"Sure, I mean if you want to," I responded hesitantly. She ordered us a buffet, then laid down on her bed and turned on a TV show.

I got up to put my PJs on in the bathroom and caught a glimpse of myself in the mirror. I felt miserable and out of place, but I didn't understand why. *How can I possibly be sad? I'm staying in the nicest hotel New York has to offer, and my best friend is my boss.* I thought to myself. *I don't deserve to feel sad.*

I went and laid down in my bed, but had a hard time falling asleep. I felt important, like my job gave me a new purpose, but I didn't feel worthy of that. Private drivers, private jets, fancy NYC hotels, this was never a part of my life before. Was I showing that I appreciated it enough? Was I working hard enough? It was so hard to tell if I was ever doing a decent enough job, which was horrifying. I couldn't bear the thought of upsetting my best friend.

The next morning, we went to meet up with Kate's manager. The driver got out to open the door for us, I thanked him and asked how his day was going. It always felt weird being waited on by these strangers without at least a little bit of conversation.

"Okay, ladies. Today is a big day," her manager told us as we headed to the event. She listed off all the important people who were going to be there and the different things they could potentially offer Kate. I felt like I was a part of this team, this family, this dream and success. I felt worthy, distinguished, needed. I didn't want that to go away, so I held tightly on with everything I could. This job gave my life meaning, and I didn't want to let anything get in the way of that. I shoved the confusing out-of-place sadness away and pretended everything was perfect. *I will make myself belong here.*

"Are you ready to go in, Jackie?"

"Yes, absolutely. Let's do this."

III

I'm fourteen years old, my dad is taking Alex and me out to the softball fields to get some practice in before high school tryouts next week. Alex made starting varsity as a freshman, so I really hope I can do that as well. I have to. If I don't, everyone will know that I'm not as good as her, and that can't happen. I feel like I have a lot to live up to in my big sister. She takes mostly AP classes, the smart ones, and has had a 4.0 all throughout high school. I don't think I'm smart enough to meet that, but I hope nobody notices.

We arrive at the field and I put on my catcher's gear since my dad wants Alex to hit first. My dad is on the pitcher's mound winding up to throw. I squat down in my position to catch. He throws the ball wild, I fall to my knees to try to block it, but I miss.

"Hey, moron, I have a whole bucket of balls up here. Sit back down!" he yells as I start to stand up to get the ball that got past me. Alex is still standing there ready to hit. She looks focused.

"Okay Al, hands up and keep your eye on this ball right here."

He throws it again, this time I catch it, but it somehow still falls out of my glove.

"Jax! Come on, you're acting like you've never even played before. What are you scared of? Don't be a moron and catch the damn ball!"

I feel myself about to start crying but pull back my tears as I've been told many times before that's not allowed. *Please hit this next one, Alex.* I think to myself, hoping for a break.

It's now my turn to hit, which I'm even worse at than catching. I conceal my fear, put on my helmet and get in the batter's box. My dad looks mad. He just finished yelling at Alex for not hitting good enough so I'm a bit worried about what this will be like. If she can't even hit today, how in the world will I be able to?

After four failed swings, I realize that I was right.

"Do you even care? Are you even listening to me? Open your eyes and hit the damn ball! It's really not that hard!" Dad yelled.

About an hour later, our practice ends, and we gather our gear to bring back to the car. I have to carry most of it since I did the worst.

I think Alex is crying, but it's hard to tell. Dad puts a different kind of pressure on her than he does on me, which I'm thankful for but a little confused by.

"Jackie, if you don't want to play in college, it's fine," Dad says as we're driving back home. "You don't have natural talent like your sister does, but I know you don't take any of this seriously anyway."

I don't respond, I just sit in silence and let him talk to Alex for the rest of the way home.

———

The clouds look extra gloomy today, I thought to myself as I stared through the fogginess covering the window inside of Tatte. I was curled up with my book in my little booth upstairs, unsure of my plans. My coffee was just about gone, and I hadn't really done much other than reading.

"Hey Jackie, what book is that?" the barista asked as she stopped by my table on her way out from her shift.

"Oh, uh, this one is Miracles by CS Lewis, and this one is Emma by Jane Austen. Have you read either of them?"

"Oh yes, yes I have! Wonderful books, enjoy! See you tomorrow?"

"I'll be here!" I said attempting to sound cheerful. I looked down at the two books sitting on my table, picked up Emma and flipped through to see how many pages I had until I was done. I have read so much of that ridiculous book, I couldn't believe how much I had left in it *still*. Nothing noteworthy had really happened that I can recall, just a lot of lengthy conversations with old words I didn't understand.

My phone buzzed. It was my boss.

"Hey, we're going to study in the dining hall tonight if you want to join us," Kate said.

"I would love to! I'm in Tatte right now, I'll head that way," I answer quickly. I was excited to be around other people in a different environment for the first time all week, even if it meant sitting in a dining hall watching everybody study for tests I didn't have to take. I gathered my books and rode my bike to the dorms.

As I waited to be let inside, I pulled up Instagram to check in on what the rest of the world was doing on this Friday night. My best friends in LA had posted a story together, all gathered around a dinner table drinking good wine and eating homemade food. They looked so happy, so full of life, far from how I felt. I would have given anything to be there.

I made it inside the dorms and down to the dining hall. Everyone was situated already with their books, laptops, and hot tea. Seated around the table, not one head looked up as I arrived. Stacks of books thicker than any I had ever owned, writing papers longer than most books I had read, and studying for tests I thanked God I didn't have to take. I quietly sought out a vacant seat and placed my bag down as gently as I could to not disturb them. I looked around me, smiled at my best friend, and pretended not to notice her choice not to smile back.

Not the slightest part of me felt worthy to be sitting at this table. What business did I have at a school as prestigious as Harvard, anyway? I had never felt like I fit in less in my life. Part of me hoped for a conversation to start eventually since that's generally one of my opportunities to at least make someone laugh, but another part of me feared being caught as the imposter I knew I was. If I talked, would they know I'm not smart enough to belong there? I might as well have the words "I don't go here" written across my forehead.

"How do you all feel about the metaphysical qualities Descartes discussed in the book we read today?"

I looked up from the book I was hiding behind, scanned the table for anyone else who might feel even slightly as confused as me from this question. No one had spoken up yet, so I still had a chance. I pulled my phone out onto my lap, typed the words "metaphysical" and "existential" into Google, and quickly tried to piece together the meaning behind what was being asked. I had nothing.

"Oh, I strongly admired his theories on existence," the girl sitting across the table from me answered after a brief moment of contemplation.

"You're not smart Jackie, you're a moron. No one here would take you seriously, everyone sees

through to the airhead you really are," my insecurities shouted at me.

Everybody nodded along, continuing to discuss this topic that I had to look up every other word for. *I'm an idiot. I do not belong here,* I thought to myself, hoping and praying with everything I had that nobody would notice my absence from the conversation. I so desperately wanted to belong at this table, but my place felt far out of reach.

"Hey, I'm going to go get a snack. Does anybody want anything?" I ask.

"Oh, yes. Would you bring us some of that cake? It was someone's birthday earlier and evidently, they forgot the leftovers."

"Absolutely," I answered as I diligently made my way over to the food table. I didn't actually want a snack. I just needed to find a way to make myself useful, or at the very least have *something* to say even if it had nothing to do with anything intellectually suitable to add to their conversation.

On my way to the snacks, I pulled out my phone and started looking up more of what the conversation was about in hopes of having an opinion of my own to bring back to the table. I could barely even pronounce the words I found, so it felt like a lost cause. I grabbed the cake for my boss, a banana for me, and headed back.

Everyone was deep into their studying again, so I put down the snacks and pulled out my Jane Austen book to try and fit in. They all loved Jane Austen, so I felt like I needed to as well. At least then maybe I could have *something* to relate on or discuss at the next study session.

Halfway through the page that I left off on earlier, I realized that I had no idea what I just read. Not just in that particular chapter, but in the whole book. I started over again.

This book is so weird, did anything even happen? I think to myself. I felt like I was back in high school.

As the night came to a close, I packed up my books and made my way back to my Airbnb. My walk felt longer than normal, and the only thoughts in my head were about how *stupid* I felt and how everyone must have known it. The apartment felt below freezing, so I slipped on my fuzzy socks and curled up on the couch. I put my book on the coffee table, turned on Parks and Rec, and began my ritual of numbing out.

IV

I'm ten years old, sitting at the kitchen table eating dinner next to my mom and dad. Chicken, rice, veggies, it's all in front of me. I take a bite of rice, and my dad asks me to stand up from the table and walk over next to him. I hesitate, unsure of what he wants, but get up and go to him as instructed.

"What is it?" I ask. He doesn't respond, but instead makes a peculiar face and puts his hands on my stomach. I feel his rough hands shift from the front of my belly to my sides, pinching around the skin on my hips.

"Hm," he mumbles as he gives me one more feel.

"What are you doing?" I ask timidly.

"Well, your mom and I saw you sitting in the hot tub at the neighbor's house and it looked like you might have gained some weight. Just wanted to check."

"Maybe it was just the way she was sitting?" my mom says from the other side of the kitchen.

I sit back down in my seat and stare at the plate full of rice and chicken in front of me. I pick up my fork to move my food around, letting my head hang down in front of me. I feel ashamed, like I did something wrong. I put down my fork, clear my plate from the table and go upstairs to my room. I'm still hungry, but I pretend I'm not.

I'm thirteen years old and just started the seventh grade. School is complicated. Sometimes I like it and sometimes I hate it. I get really scared to talk to the other girls because I'm not sure if they like me. They're all really pretty and the boys seem to like them a lot. I don't think boys like me.

I'm at dinner with my parents after school. My mom made chicken and rice again, a meal I normally love. I look down at my plate to see all the rice, but I don't think I'm allowed to eat it. I look over at my sister, she seems to be eating the meal okay. I look at my mom and notice her moving the rice around on her plate as well, similar to what I was doing.

My mom gets up to go to the bathroom, and my dad starts talking to my sister. Now is my chance. I grab a napkin from the counter, sit back down and take a huge bite of chicken. Nobody is looking at me, so I pick up the napkin as if I'm wiping my mouth, and then spit my bite into it instead. I hide my filled napkin on my lap under the table, and slowly lift my head up to see if anyone noticed. I'm safe.

Dad keeps talking to Alex and mom is starting to clean the kitchen, so I realize this is my chance. I get up to grab more napkins, sit back down and continue to spit out my bites till most of my food is gone. I stand up, put my *empty-enough* plate in the sink, throw away my filled-up napkins and go upstairs into my room. I sit on my bed, look down at my empty stomach, and sigh from relief. I am okay.

I'm 19 now, and currently have my job working as a personal assistant to that musician, Steve, in LA. Part of my job lately is cooking meals for him every day. He gives me his credit card, I go buy all the groceries, then come back to his apartment to prepare the meals. I do this for both lunch and dinner, sometimes breakfast too.

"Jax, come get your two bites before it's all gone!" Steve yells from the other room while I'm in the kitchen cleaning the dishes. I wipe off my hands and walk into his room where he's sitting at his desk. I grab his fork, take a little bite of the noodles on his plate, and soak in the warmth of the food in my mouth.

"Wow, you're so skinny today, Jax!" my boss says as he pulls me towards himself and feels around my stomach. He seems to be really happy that I'm skinny, like it's something I'm doing *for him*.

"Thank you," I say, unsure of what the proper response is. I am still hungry, but I pretend not to be. All I've eaten this week has been bananas and cereal, but I ignore my desire for real food and let Steve admire my body instead. I feel as if it belongs to him now, not me.

"Okay, Jax. I got to get some work done. Can you do some laundry?" he says as he pushes me away.

"Yeah, of course."

I walk into his closet, grab his dirty clothes pile and take it into the laundry room. The whole way there, I feel highly aware of my body. My boss makes comments about it more than regularly.

"Wow Jackie, you used to be so much thicker and I was so sad, but now you're skinny! You look amazing. Whatever you're doing, keep doing it," are comments he's made while I've been working for him. I can't go back to being *thicker*.

———

Kate and I just got back to Boston from another trip to New York City, and were riding in our car from the train station to the dorms. I felt tired and weak but continued trying to make conversation with the driver to break the silence.

"Jackie, I'm starving. I need a meal. Are you cool with going to Tatte for dinner before we go home?" my best friend asked.

"Yeah, totally," I answered.

Our driver dropped us off and pulled around to the side to wait for us to be done.

"Just text me when you girls are done, and I'll swing back around to pick you up."

We rushed inside to escape the cold and put our bags down on a table to save. Tatte felt warm and much less crowded at this time of night.

"What do you think you're gonna get, Jackie?"

"I'm actually okay, I think I'm just gonna get a tea. I have some cereal at home that I've been craving all day.

"Are you sure?"

"I'm positive."

"Well do you at least want to share with me?"

"Yeah, I guess I can do that," I answered. I didn't want to draw any more attention to myself, so agreeing to share felt easier than not.

We sat back down at our table as a barista brought our food over. Kate grabbed a spoon and dug in. She was really hungry. So was I. I watched her eat the meal we agreed to share, picked up my tea and started to talk about how great our New York trip was.

"Yeah, it was great. But Jackie, don't you want to eat any of this?"

"Yeah! Of course," I said as I picked up a spoon and grabbed a little bite for myself. I was starving, and this food was incredibly delicious, but I didn't feel capable of eating it. I didn't think I was supposed to. Eating real meals was okay for everyone else, but I remembered that I was different.

I got up to go to the bathroom and stared at myself in the mirror. My body didn't look familiar anymore, and I couldn't quite figure out why. Something was off, and I was so weak and tired and just wanted to go to bed. I was so hungry.

I left the bathroom and walked back over to Kate who was still enjoying the meal we were supposed to be sharing. I sat down and immediately changed the subject once more as I picked up my spoon to move around my side of the meal, attempting to make it seem like I was participating.

"Jackie, what did you eat today?" she asked, completely undistracted from my failed attempts to change of subject.

"Oh, you know! The normal Jackie G meals. I had a protein shake, then one of those granola bars."

"That's all you ate? And you're not eating now?" she asked, looking away from me as if she was deeply processing what I was saying. It was as if it didn't make sense to her. It definitely made sense to me. It was my life. I understood it. But her being uncomfortable with that made me uncomfortable, so I changed the subject again. This time, she let me.

I got back to my Airbnb that night, looked at the cereal I claimed to crave sitting on top of my fridge, and grabbed an apple instead. I cut it in half, just like my mom always did growing up, and went to lay down in bed. I opened up my computer, went to an episode of Friends, and finally let myself cry. I felt around my wrists, pinched the skin on my hips, and felt like I wanted to slip out of my body.

"Nothing is mine," I whispered. I didn't feel familiar. I felt like a prisoner trapped inside my skin, and I hated everything that I felt. I was so hungry. I couldn't remember a time when I wasn't. But I still felt too big. I still felt like the only way to get through this life was to be small.

I finished my apple, jumped out of bed and ran into the bathroom. I opened the lid to the toilet and grabbed my toothbrush from the sink. I knew what to do. I had seen it on TV and read about it online. I stuck my toothbrush down to the back of my throat, closed my eyes, and tried to make myself throw up. Nothing came out. I tried it again, but this time it hurt too much so I stopped.

Tears started pouring out of my eyes, I dropped my toothbrush on the floor and grabbed a tissue from the counter. I felt like a failure. I couldn't even make myself throw up.

I picked myself up from the floor, walked into my room and curled up inside my bed.

"I'm going to be okay. I'm going to get through this," I whispered as I pressed play on the episode of Friends waiting for me. My mind turned away from myself, onto the show, and I closed my eyes to fall asleep and start over again the next day.

It was pouring rain outside. I was riding my bike quickly to the local yoga studio to get into class on time. I kept my head down as I pushed open the front door to check in at the desk.

"We're in room 2 on your left, Jackie, I'll see you in there!" The lady said with a smile.

I forced a grin back then headed to the locker room to put my shoes in a cubby. I took off my jacket and considered my shirt as well, that's what most people seem to be doing. *No way, not going to happen.*

I walked into the studio. There was a big mirror covering the wall up front, most of the other people in the class had gathered up close. They all looked at their reflections, making sure their hair was pulled back right and their stretches were properly formed. I brought my mat to the farthest back corner available, far out of view, and sat myself down.

"I don't want them to see me, I don't want the teacher to see me, and most of all I don't want to risk being forced to see myself."

Mirrors were my enemy. Mirrors showed me what I hated, what I didn't want to be aware of. They showed me myself, my body, my broken eyes and hurting soul. I didn't like myself.

The teacher walked in and turned on the lights, which made my reflection more difficult to avoid. The class began in a mountain pose, and we were instructed to keep our eyes closed. *One, two, three.* I breathed in deeply, I felt safe when my eyes were shut.

"Okay class open your eyes once you're ready," she instructed.

My stomach started to knot up. I wasn't ready for this. Yoga was supposed to be an escape, who in their right mind would put a giant mirror in here? I wanted to leave, I didn't want to see me.

I opened my eyes, and there staring back at me was myself. I looked sad, I looked tired, I looked broken. There was no power there. I moved my gaze to focus on the floor in front of me, counting down the minutes till class was over.

I don't like me.

V

I'm 17 years old. My best friend, Suzy, is pregnant, and I'm really excited to be an aunt. She's not my real big sister, but she calls herself one and tells me I'm her little sister, so I believe her. Suzy has been my best friend for about a year now, and I really don't know what I would do without her. Sometimes she gets really mad at me, but she's pregnant so I just blame it on the hormones. After all, I have no idea what it's like to be pregnant. Maybe I'd be mean too.

I really like her boyfriend. He calls himself my big brother, which I really like. I've always wanted a big brother. I feel really safe with both of them, and we're all planning on moving out soon into our own apartment. I can't wait for that to happen because I really can't stand my real family. They hate my Suzy and her boyfriend because they think they're bad influences. It makes sense in a way. I mean, I did smoke my first bowl of weed with Suzy, in a church parking lot of all places. But my life seems like it has more purpose with their approval.

She's really cool, kind of like the girls on TV. She is bold, unapologetic, confident, and parties a lot.

I don't really drink yet, but I want to. I mostly just smoke a lot of weed. I really want to be like her. She seems to know more about life than me. I have a lot to learn.

Suzy is mad at me today, and it makes me really upset. I don't feel okay when she doesn't feel okay. When she is kind and loving towards me, I feel like I'm on top of the world. Then I am good enough, accepted, like I belong and have a purpose. But when she decides she's not happy with me, as she does often, I feel like my identity is gone. I'm not good enough and I'm not worthy.

I'm at school right now, and I look down at my phone to a text from Suzy. She's in the hospital. Something's wrong with the baby.

I jump out of my seat, ask to be excused to go to the bathroom, run to my car and head to the hospital. I can't breathe, I feel like my heart is stopping. This baby has to be okay, she just has to. We have plans of raising her. We bought her all her baby clothes and made plans to paint her room. I was going to be the best aunt in the world, and we were all going to live together. But what if she's not okay? What does that mean for my best friend? What does that mean for her boyfriend? Will they be okay? I can barely handle this heaviness and I'm not even one of the parents. I can't handle this.

I pull up in front of the hospital, grab my bags and run toward the front door. I hate hospitals, but that doesn't matter right now. I had a test today, but that doesn't matter either. The only thing that matters is this baby.

I make it upstairs to her room, slowly crack open the door and see her laying in the hospital bed on the other side of the room. She looks weak and scared, unlike I've ever seen her before. Normally she looks bold and brave, confident that she could take over the world if she wanted to. But right now, I've never seen vulnerable look so real.

"Hey Jax, thanks for coming," Suzy says with her eyes half open. I can tell she's been crying, and I hate that there's nothing I can do to take away her pain. I don't have words, and that makes me feel unworthy of being here. I can't fix it.

"Hey! There you are, Jackpot," her boyfriend says smiling as he walks in the room. He calls me Jackpot. "Do you want anything to eat? I'm running over to Taco Bell."

"I'm okay, thank you though." He walks over to give me a hug, and I run out of things to say. Silently, I hug him back.

Suzy starts crying from pain, and a nurse comes in to give her an epidural.

"We're going to need everyone to clear the room except for the father," the nurse says with a sudden urgency in her voice. I grab my bag, stand up from my chair and nervously make my way to the waiting area outside. As I leave, I pass by three more doctors rushing into her room to help. She's having her baby, right now, this is happening.

I sit down on a chair in the hallway, hold my chin in my hands that are resting on my knees. I look down at the floor, counting the little pieces of dust next to my feet. I pull my head up to see my best friend's mom and dad sitting across from me, all of us unsure as to whether or not we should stand and greet each other. Silence fills the room, and we wait to be told what to do next.

We hear a door open across the hall, and I look over to see my "big brother" standing outside the door, wiping his eyes with his hand. Something isn't right. I get out of my seat, run over to where he's standing and beg for information.

"What happened? Is she okay? Is the baby okay?" I plead.

"No," he says as he starts to cry again and grabs onto me for comfort, "Nobody is okay. The baby died."

I walk into the room, pull back my tears, bite my tongue, and see my best friend holding her dead child on the bed. The room is quiet, nobody is saying a word and Suzy has a blank stare on her face. She's not crying, but I know she isn't okay.

"Will you hold her?" my best friend asks me. I'm unsure of what to say, nobody has ever asked me to hold their dead child before and it scares me for obvious reasons. I don't feel capable of holding something so fragile and sacred, but the last thing I want to do is say or do the wrong thing.

"Yes, of course," I answer as I reach my arms out to cradle her baby. I'm not sure what I'm supposed to do next, so I rock her back and forth and kiss her forehead. Finally, the tears come.

A doctor comes into the room and asks for the baby. They need to take pictures of her body. I'm not entirely sure why. I hand over my dead niece to the doctor, and watch them unroll her from the blankets that she is wrapped in. They lay her on the bed, pulling her little arms up so they can get a good photo, followed by her legs and head. She's so small, so helpless, I'm afraid they're going to break her.

It's getting late now, and visiting hours are about to end. I pick up my things, hug my best friend, feel shame for the lack of words I'm able to give her as encouragement, and leave. I walk outside, get in my car, light up my pipe and smoke a bowl of weed. Nothing is okay, nothing is the same, and I have no idea how I'm supposed to handle this. I'm supposed to be a better friend than this, I'm supposed to have the right things to say but I don't. If I can't comfort my best friend, what am I even there for? What is my purpose? There is nothing I can do to take away this pain from any of them. I feel useless.

In silence, I drive home, crawl into bed, and lay with my eyes closed unable to fall asleep till morning came.

———

I woke early one morning, as I generally do when I feel out of place. The heater broke in my Airbnb last night, my toes were so cold they were curled underneath each other under my covers to de-frost. I rolled over onto my side to grab my phone and see what time it was: 6 am. There was no going back to sleep now so I anxiously slid myself out of bed and into the bathroom.

Staring at myself in the mirror, I remembered I ate more than I was supposed to in the dining hall the night before, so I pulled my hair back tight and decided to go on a run. It was too cold on a morning like this in Boston, but I put on as many layers as I could find and forced myself to go anyway.

The bitterness of the air pierced my cheeks the second I stepped outside. Running this early, in this uncomfortably cold weather made no sense at all. But I didn't have a choice.

Normally running helped me decompress from my mind quite a bit, but not that time. All I could think about was Kate, extremely concern that she was mad at me. She wasn't really talking to me the day before, and I couldn't quite figure out why, or what I could have done to upset her. Normally she was fine, we had never been in a fight before, but everything I seemed to do lately made her upset. I know that she has a lot of school work to do so I hope I haven't been a distraction. When I first got here, I was told that I needed to be careful of that since this was her senior year. I needed to make sure not to be around all the time, to give her space to be with her school friends. I really hope I haven't overstepped.

It has felt so complicated being best friends with my boss. Especially when my job is being on call most of the time. They still haven't quite told me what my duties are, and I don't want to risk not being available if I'm needed. I want to do a good job at being an assistant, I want to be a good best friend, but I also want to give her space.

These thoughts dictated my mental space for most of my run, so I decided to turn around and go home to start the rest of my day. It was only about 6:45 am, but I felt too anxious about being potentially needed and unavailable.

I made it back to my Airbnb to change, and instantly turned back around to ride my bike to Tatte. The barista saw me walking in, smiled and tried to make conversation. However, I couldn't seem to get my social skills to work, which felt ironic because of how badly I craved a meaningful conversation. Every question I thought I could ask felt annoying, so I ordered my coffee as quickly as I could and went to sit down in my booth by the window. That booth was the only safe place I could find in the whole city of Boston. I opened my book, put my feet up on the chair in front of me, and began my escape.

Many hours later, I got a text from my boss letting me know her dog died. She is not okay. I instantly felt helpless, unable to do anything to take her pain away. I panicked. *If I can't help, what good am I? Will she be mad that I can't help?*

"Do you need anything? Is there anything I can do? I'm so sorry!!" I text back.

"No, I just needed to tell you," she responded. That wasn't good enough for me, and I began to panic.

I left the coffee shop and rode my bike through the rain to the nearest flower store I could find. I knew I was going to see her later at a church group, and I couldn't show up empty-handed.

There they were, white roses, those were the flowers I needed to get. I didn't have enough cash on me, so I grabbed my credit card and slammed it on the checkout counter in a hurry.

"These are such beautiful roses!" the clerk said with a big smile. "Are these all for you today, miss?"

"Yes, that's all," I said quickly as I wrapped the roses up in my arms and made my way to my best friend.

I unlocked my bike, gently placed the flowers in the front basket and hastily rode down the street to where the church group was being held. The door wasn't unlocked yet and I didn't have a card to swipe myself in, so I waited outside in the cold.

About ten minutes went by until someone finally noticed I needed to be let in. I urgently grabbed my things and found a warm spot on the couch. My best friend was already in there with her other friends, and we made eye contact for a brief moment before she realizes she forgot I was coming.

I felt inextricably uncomfortable, still unsure if she wanted me to be there or not. I shook off my anxiety, grabbed my white roses and walked over to hand them to Kate.

"Hey, I got you these. I'm so sorry about your dog, I know you said I didn't need to do anything, but I just really wanted to."

"Oh, well thank you, Jackie. That's very kind of you," she said as we began to walk into the service. She put the flowers down on the side table with the rest of her things and sat down on a chair in the front. I wasn't sure if she wanted me to sit by her or not, so I lingered around in the back and pretended to have interest in the snack table for a while.

After about an hour, church ended, and the small talk begins. Normally I'm great at all sorts of conversation, but my insecurities felt much louder than my charisma. I looked up to see if my best friend was still there; I really wanted to make sure she wasn't mad at me before the day ended, but also just to see if she was okay.

"Jackie! I feel like I haven't seen you in so long, how are you?" one of our friends asked as she grabbed my arm to pull me into a hug.

"I'm great! Boston has been so pretty. It's just cold!" I answer with a response I know is safe from any level of vulnerability.

My best friend saw me talking to our friend and walked over to join the conversation.

"Hey guys," she says as she puts her arm around my shoulder and leans her head against mine, finally acknowledging that I was there.

"Oh, look at you pretty girl, where'd you get your flowers?" our friend asked her.

"Oh, Jackie gave them to me."

"Awe! That is so sweet of Jackie to do that!"

"Yeah, it was," Kate said as she pulled me to the side. "Hey, I'm gonna start walking back to my dorm."

"Oh, okay! I was planning on heading out too. Can I walk with you?"

"Yeah, sure," she answered with her head down. On our way out, different people came up to ask her where the flowers came from. As a joke, she started to hand out individual roses to everyone who passed by.

"Here, you can have one," she says as she tried to get out of the door.

I was sad that she gave my gift away right in front of me but thankful to get the chance to walk back with her, hoping that it would open up a conversation that might need to be had. If I was doing something wrong, I wanted to know, but also desperately felt like I needed to be there for her if she needed me after her dog died.

As we left the building, she got on the phone with her mom. They talked for the majority of the walk home, and I followed behind waiting for further instructions.

There was so much in me that felt like in order to be okay, in order to have a purpose and be needed, I needed to be able to be available in this for my friend. I needed to be needed, I needed to help, be useful, whatever that looked like.

We got back to her dorm, said our goodbyes, and I grabbed my bike and began to make my way home. I didn't have the words to fix it.

"I'm a failure," I mumbled under my breath.

VI

"If you died right now, are you 100% positive that you would go to heaven?" my dad asks me at about twelve years old.

"Uhm, I don't really know," I answer timidly, feeling dumb for not just pretending to know and avoid the embarrassment.

"Well, then you better figure it out," he responds with a stern look of intimidation across his face.

I believed God was real growing up, at least I think I did. My dad made God really scary and unappealing to Alex and me, so I didn't really want much to do with it. But if you asked me back then, I would have told you "I'm a Christian!" in the same way that I would have said, "I'm an American!"

At age 19, I began my own faith journey apart from my parents. Now I just turned twenty-one, and I'm really involved at a very trendy church in LA. It's somewhat of a megachurch, and our Pastor is famous enough to need a green room. I initially started coming to this church because my boss wanted to. He called it "the church of the stars" since it's where people like Justin Bieber goes. Everyone there is dressed in leather jackets, skinny jeans, and shoes that look more expensive than my car. I'm trying to be as involved as I can, so I volunteer as a greeter, help host a community group, and hang out with everyone from the church as often as possible. I love it there, especially the group. It's where I feel like I belong.

Everyone who I'm friends with from church seems to know more than me, though. They were all raised in church, and I wasn't. I wish I was, I feel shame over my story and how rebellious it is compared to everyone else's. Most of them call me a "baby Christian" and tell me how great my childlike faith is. I don't often feel capable of doing much more than just asking them questions.

The leader of our community group is my ex-boss and sister's ex-boyfriend. It feels weird that he's leading the group. A lot of the time it feels like it's more about him than a Bible study. He invites his fans from Instagram sometimes, and they all gush over the fact that he's *somewhat* famous on the internet. That drives me crazy. A few of my close friends stopped coming to group a while ago because of him, and I don't really blame them. I feel so mad at him most of the time, but also still feel like I need him to approve of me.

It's been about a year and a half since he first kissed me on that tour, the one where I slept outside on the ground because of how ashamed I was. I'm still so angry at him for that, and he kept telling me not to tell anyone, that it's something that should just stay between the two of us because no one will understand. He doesn't understand why people would be mad, even my sister. It's eating me alive.

Throughout the year and a half, we never actually dated. He would constantly be going back and forth with whether or not he wanted to be with me, never fully acknowledging whether I wanted to or not. It was practically a one-sided conversation he was having with himself. However, the other day when we were shopping at Target, he apparently made up his mind and asked me to be his girlfriend. I told him no.

"Wow, you're the first girl that's ever said no to me! I'm proud of you, my mom would be proud of you too," he responded.

He's gone on tour now, thank goodness. I finally have time to detach from him and get my head straight. His attention feels like a drug sometimes, so a detox feels necessary. Two girls just started coming to our group, and I really like them. They've been so above and beyond kind to me, and I feel really special when they want to spend time together. They both grew up in church and were a few years older, so I trust them with a lot. They call me their sister, which makes me feel special.

"Hey, can you guys drive me back to my apartment after group? I need to talk to you about something," I ask.

"Of course!"

All together in one car pulling up to my apartment, my chest is pounding. I know I need to tell someone about my boss, who was also the leader of this Bible study, and now is the perfect chance. He's gone, they barely know him, and they seem to really care about me so now is my shot. Telling the story about what happened with my boss and I is by far the most shameful and terrifying thing that I have ever imagined doing. It's the story that I believe is what makes me unlovable. But I'm really involved in church now, and every time I hear a sermon about honesty, I want to be sick. There have been so many moments where my stomach curls and my heart burns, like I am the only exception to this whole *grace* thing. I'm so terrified this is what will send me to hell. I need somebody to help me, to tell me that I'm still loved and still okay.

"Okay, what is it, Jackie?" they ask. A few moments of silence pass by before I'm finally able to get the words out. "You don't have to be scared to tell us, we love you," they assure me.

"Okay. This isn't easy to tell you, but things have been going on between Steve and I," I say with shakiness in my voice. They don't say much, so I continue to tell them the rest of the story. I tell them about the tour, about the drunk *mistakes*, about how much I hated myself to the very core, and how I could never be with him but feel so attached still.

"Well Jackie, I'm not happy that you lied to us. Thank you for sharing and being honest. It's going to be okay. Can we pray for you?"

They put their hands on me and say a long prayer with very big spiritual words. I don't know what half of them mean, but it sounds important. I'm not sure if I feel better or worse, but at least I told them.

It's been about a week since I told my two friends my story, and now my boss is coming home from tour. I really don't want him to be back. I'm still not done detoxing from his narcissistic personality. But he's back now, and I am determined that things will be different.

We have community group tonight and I'm home getting ready right now. My phone buzzes and I look down to see my friends texting me, the ones who I shared my story with.

"Are you good to do dinner with all of us tonight before group? We need to talk about things," the message says. I respond and agree to meet, not entirely sure what's going on. It feels a little weird that they want to meet with my boss and I, kind of like an intervention or something. But it's okay, I trust them.

They pull up to my apartment to pick me up, and I get in the car to find that my boss is already there. Apparently, they spent the day together doing some photoshoot. That makes me feel really weird, but I don't want them to know that. I need to be cool about this. The car feels awkward though, like I'm the only person who's not entirely in the loop. We arrive at the restaurant and all sit down around a table with our food. After a few minutes of small talk, they get down to business.

My boss speaks up first. I can't really look at him; the table feels intense and I'm not sure what he's about to say. I'm confused as to why we're all here. I already told him I couldn't be with him when he asked me before he left on his tour, but here we are again.

"Jackie, there's just so much that's special about you," he says. He goes on for a while about his story from growing up, insecurities he's had, his long string of dysfunctional relationships, then asks me to be together once more.

I don't say anything. I feel as if somehow, I lost the ability to speak, or do anything else other than stare down at the table in front of me.

"Jackie," my friend says sternly, "tell him what you told us."

I take a deep breath, I feel as if this has been the longest dinner of my life. How did I even get here? Why are they doing this to me? He knows how I feel, I already told him. Does my *no* not mean anything at all?

"Jackie, tell him," she says again. I look up from the table, look my boss in the eyes, and gather the courage to speak.

"I can't be with you." I did it. I can't believe I was finally able to say that. I feel like I should be excited, but for some reason, I feel numb. He's crying hard now, and my friends start to comfort him. One gets up to get him a Kleenex, and the other tells him she wants to connect him with her dad to help him through this hard time. I'm now alone on my side of the table, and stare back down at the untouched plate of food in front of me.

"Okay, are you all ready to go now? We need to get back for group," my friend announces as she stands up from the table. We don't answer, but we all stand up and follow her out to the car. My two friends walk ahead of my boss and I, talking amongst themselves. Are we supposed to be talking, too? Is this part of it? I am beyond uncomfortable.

We all get in the car that we conveniently rode in together, and drive to the community group that we're all a part of. Is this supposed to feel this uncomfortable?

The group is ending now, and I am not okay. I stay behind and make small talk with the others so I can wait for my two friends. I really need to talk to them; I have not felt *this* not okay in a long, long time. One by one people start to clear out of the apartment, and my two friends go into my boss's room alone with him and close the door. I'm bothered by this, but I don't want them to know that. I just need my friends.

It's getting late now and they still haven't come out, so I think I should start to head home. I only live a few buildings away, so I walk. As soon as I step into my apartment, the heaviness of my heartache takes over. I run into my room, fall onto my bed and burst into tears. I'm crying loudly and feel like I can't breathe. My roommate knocks on my door to see if I'm okay, but I'm embarrassed and confused so I tell her I'm fine.

I pick up my phone to text my friends. I know I'm not okay, and maybe even just if they come over and prayed for me it would help?

"Hey, if you guys are still at the apartment, do you think you can come over on your way out just to pray for me? I'm really not okay," I text them.

They respond telling me that they are too drained, and don't want to pray from a place of resentment. I throw my phone across the room and cry myself to sleep.

It's been a few days since the dinner from hell, and I learn that my two friends had started a band with my boss that night after group. They haven't really spoken to me since, and word is starting to get out about what happened. I'm on my way to meet another one of my close friends who found out about Steve and me for coffee, but she's acting strange.

"Jackie, I wrote you a letter that I am going to read out loud to you," she says.

I keep my head down, fully ashamed to even be existing right now. I feel like I just ruined everyone's life by being a part of them, and there's no way out of this.

Her letter is long, it talks about how much I hurt her and that she can't trust me anymore. She writes that I need to find a new community group, and my boss should stay in the original one because he really needs his friends right now. But I need to find a new one, and she offers to go to one with me but then reminds me that we're not friends anymore. Yeah. Word got out.

"You can keep the letter," she says as she finishes and passes it down to my side of the table. I'm crying now and so is she. She was another one of my best friends, one who always wanted to pray for me and have deep life talks with.

I get in my car and make my drive home. I cry the whole way and continue as I fall onto my bed. I hate myself. I need my friends, I need my church, but I'm not welcome there anymore.

I'm twenty-two now, and I just moved to Nashville to go to a ministry school. That's what I've been telling people anyway. In all honesty, I just needed to start over. I'm so hurt by what happened in

LA with my boss and community group, I needed out.

I haven't been to Nashville in a while and don't really know anybody here. But I think that's a good thing. Ministry school is interesting. I'm not so sure how I feel about everything they're teaching there, but everyone is telling me to stay teachable and to not be a skeptic. They have us play these "prophetic games" where we run around telling everyone what God is saying about them, or what superhero God thinks they are. It feels weird, but I guess I'll just stay teachable.

This week, they're giving us a lesson called "why our church is so weird." I'm excited about that, maybe this will make me not feel so confused about this place. I want to like ministry school so bad, but it feels really weird claiming God is saying all these things to me about people that may or may not be true. I believe God speaks to me, but I feel like this isn't right. God isn't a puppet, I don't think any random thought that goes through my head is from him, and I don't like people telling me things about myself that may or may not be true that they think God told them. One of my roommates told me that God told her she should have the bigger room, and she is going to get married at twenty-three. That doesn't feel right to me.

The main thing I want answers for is this thing they call "manifestations." That's when they claim that the Holy Spirit takes over their bodies making them fall over and roll around on the ground or shake uncontrollably or make animal noises. They also scream and cackle and laugh, and it really scares me. But I really want to belong, and I'm hopeful that this lesson called "why our church is so weird" will help give me peace about all of this.

There's a guest speaker for this session who I have never heard of but everyone else seems to love.

"Everybody! Stand up if you've ever felt tormented by dark thoughts in your mind!" he demands. I look around me and see practically the whole room stand up, so I feel safe to do so too.

He starts praying, loudly, calling the evil spirits out of everyone standing up. I hear a scream from the back of the room and turn around to see what happened. Another scream, this one louder, comes from the other side. The room is incredibly loud now with laughing and screaming and crying and moaning. I look to my left and see one of my friends collapse to the floor as if someone threw her down. She's convulsing as if she's having a seizure, and I panic thinking I have to do something. I sit on the ground and try to calm her down, but she won't stop convulsing.

I sit down on the ground and hide my face in between my knees, feeling like I'm trapped in some kind of horror movie. I expect the speaker to do something, but he's just standing up there praying and talking about demonic spirits. I am terrified.

The session finally ends, everyone is exhausted, and we're released for lunch. I spend my lunch break crying in the bathroom.

Lunch ends and the next session starts.

"Alright! Now that we've emptied you all out, it's time to fill you back up with the Holy Spirit! Line up against the wall! Girls first, guys are going to run up and pray for you all," the guest speaker says. I've seen YouTube videos of this, and instantly tense up.

The girls line up, and as soon as the boys start praying for us the room grows loud again. There's an old CCM song playing in the background, but we can barely hear it over the screams. My body is petrified; this needs to end now. The boys are getting closer to my end of the line, and I don't want them to touch me. I don't want to be prayed for.

"Be filled with the Holy Spirit!" he yells in my face as he tries to push me down. I plant my feet firmly into the ground and refuse to let my body be manipulated into whatever this is.

He's gone now. Anxiety has fully taken over my body and I can't stop crying. I cover my face with my hands and pretend I'm anywhere else. I move my hands away to see if I can make it to the exit without being noticed, and I see my school pastor quickly making her way over to me. Everyone has moved to a different side of the room, so I'm alone in my corner.

"Jackie, what is wrong with you? What trauma from your past is this triggering?" she asks me.

"I just feel overwhelmed. All of this is so much!"

"Think hard! What trauma is this triggering to make you respond in this way?"

"I really don't think there's anything. This is just freaking me out," I answer, stammering for words.

The session is finally over, and I grab my backpack and run to the exit. I'm free. In my car I continue to cry, I can't handle this tension. I moved here for this school. This is where I'm supposed to find my home and my belonging, but I have never felt more spiritually traumatized in my life. All these people say they're Christians, they're saying that all of these disturbing "manifestations" are from Jesus. If all of this is true, I don't know if I really am a Christian after all. I don't know if I even want to be one, or if the Jesus I've been talking to for the past two years is even real. I'm so scared I'm losing who I am. I'm scared I'm wrong. I don't fit into this world.

———

Holding my backpack tightly to my chest, I watched the clusters of students pour down the escalators on their way to the train. They all looked late for something, so I pretended to as well. My backpack was stuffed with books I was supposed to be reading but didn't have the energy for, and wearing it was starting to give me back pains. All the Harvard students wore their backpacks like it was their job, so I felt like I needed one too.

It's dark inside the subway station. Part of me liked it; I felt more sane there. The gloominess matched my spirit in an uncomfortable way, but at least it felt honest. The floors were sticky, the walls needed a paint job, but no one seemed to notice.

Church was tonight, which gave me hope. It was helpful having somewhere to be, but also unhelpful at the same time for being around people that knew me as *happy*. I felt like I was slowly breaking, my body wearing down losing energy and life and breath. But I knew that church was supposed to be safe, so I waited underground for the train that would take me there.

The train arrived promptly, the doors opened and the passengers needing to exit did, and the people waiting to get on took their seats. I was the last to get on and took a seat in the back that I remembered

I had sat on before. Familiar was always helpful on the dark days.

The train arrived on time, and I got out and made my way to my church. I had never been to a church like this one before, so small and traditional. The only churches I had been to were huge, trendy, and pastored by someone with millions of followers on Instagram. This church felt more authentic, so I hoped I would get closer to finding what I was looking for there.

Social anxiety took over as soon as the first person inside said hello. People were what I knew I needed but somehow what feared the most. There weren't many people inside, maybe twenty or thirty, and I felt like the spotlight was on me. I was tired, weak, and needed anything to breathe life into me.

My faith didn't feel the same as it used to. It's still there. I mean, I hadn't written "I trust you Jesus" more in my journal more than I had there in Boston. But I felt like I lacked the ability to talk about it. There was faith I knew I was supposed to have, knowledge about theology I needed to participate in the discussions at church, but I couldn't do it. My voice was gone.

My body felt heavy, and the darkness had fully taken over my head. In every conversation, I looked for my loophole to get out. I didn't think anyone actually wanted to talk to me, so I felt like I was doing them a favor by leaving. Service was about to start, and I found a spot to sit in the back by myself. I picked my legs up onto the pew and held tightly to my knees as I listened to the sermon.

My mind was wandering, all I could do was look out the window and cry. I didn't want anyone to ask me what was wrong because I didn't know what to tell them. Everyone there expected me to be happy, to catch up on the week, but I couldn't do it. Nobody here actually knew me, and if they did, they wouldn't want to.

Service was almost over, and the pastor was taking prayer requests. One by one, people started raising their hands. Medical issues, financial burdens, family tensions, people were putting their hearts out and expecting something in return. I think they were looking for the same kind of comfort that I was. My heart started racing as I knew they were nearing the end, I so badly wanted to raise my hand and ask for prayer. But what for? I felt like I wanted to kill myself, that's what for. But if I said that they would think I was crazy or dramatic or didn't have enough faith.

Sitting and waiting, I remembered a moment with my sister and dad from growing up. My sister was telling my dad about how she struggled with anxiety before she got out of the car. Once she was gone, my dad turned to me and said, "you don't struggle with any of that stuff, you have too much faith for that." He couldn't have been more wrong.

I so badly wanted to belong here, find sanctuary here, but I wouldn't let my real soul be seen. Suddenly, my hand shot up.

"Jackie," the pastor on stage said, "what can we pray for you for?"

It all happened too quickly for me to gather my thoughts. *What was I thinking? Why did I raise my hand?* It all felt like a terrible plan but now I was stuck. *"Tell them you're depressed! Tell them you want to kill yourself and need help, it's an emergency!"* I thought to myself.

"Will you pray for my family?"

"Of course."

I lied. I couldn't do it. My life was falling apart beneath my feet, every morning and night I daydreamed about what it would be like to die. But I told them I just had family problems. This place was supposed to love me, accept me, and heal me. Why was I so terrified to be honest?

The prayer began, and tears began to pour down my cheeks. My eyes were closed, and legs hugged tightly to my chest when I felt someone grab my knee. I look up, and the pastor's wife was there in front of me. I couldn't help but smile; this was the most not alone I had felt in months. Something about her touch, something about her prayer gave me hope.

The prayer ended, she took her hand off my knee and went back to her seat. I felt cold again, lonely again, and snuck out the back door to catch the train back home.

VII

I'm 17 years old. It's been about two weeks since my best friend lost her baby. She hasn't talked to me in a while, and I'm not really sure how to fix that. I feel so helpless not knowing the right words to comfort her, so uneducated about how to talk about trauma and pain.

I'm at work right now, trying to keep myself busy. I work a lot these days because I'm not really sure what else to do. She used to work here, too. But ever since she got pregnant, she hasn't really been around, which I understand. Her boyfriend works often, though; he likes to keep himself busy and distracted in a similar way that I do. He doesn't like to talk about his pain, which I understand even more. I don't like to talk about mine either.

My shift is almost up, and I walk over through the aisles of tables to find my friends. My best friend's boyfriend stops me to ask if he can use me to be his designated driver that night, as he points over to the table he was at with some other servers who just got off. They were all headed to a bar up the street, so I guess I'd be tagging along to help get everyone home safely after. I've never really spent time in a bar before so I'm a little nervous, but I trust who I'm with so I think I'll be okay.

"Yeah, sure," I answer.

"Perfect. Thanks so much, Jackpot," he says before being interrupted by a call from his girlfriend.

I hear fighting, so I grab a broom and try to make myself look busy without having to go too far. I'm not entirely sure what's going on, but he seems really angry.

"Jackie, you're free to clock out whenever you need to," my manager says as she walks by me as I pretend to look busy.

"Jackpot, you ready?" my *big brother* asks as he gets off the phone and overhears my manager telling me to clock out.

"Yeah, let's go."

I grab my purse, put on my coat, and follow him out the door to his car. He starts the car, checks his mirrors and backs up to head to the bar. I'm not old enough to drink yet, so I'm not really sure what I'm going to do there. But I think most of the other servers are also going, so I'm sure I'll be okay.

"Alright, lil sis, I'm glad you're with me. Thanks for coming. I need this," he says.

We walk inside the bar, and he instantly sees all these old high school friends of his and leaves me sitting at the bar top to go talk to them. I feel uncomfortable, so I move over to one of the high-top tables and wait for someone I know to come sit with me.

Feeling a little awkward, I pull out my phone to appear busier than I am. My best friend is texting me, long messages about how much pain she's in. About how upset with her boyfriend she is for not being with her tonight, and how she feels like her world is falling apart. I try to understand. I try to respond with the right words, but I feel so unqualified for a conversation like this. She's 18, I'm only 17. She normally gets annoyed with me when I don't have the right words to say, so I feel scared. My heart is broken for her, for her baby, for everyone. I don't know how to fix this.

Finally, it's the last call. We say our goodbyes and walk outside. My best friend's boyfriend is stumbling, and I am anxious. I walk over to the driver's side, fully aware that my point for tagging along was to be the designated driver so he could freely drink his pain away. I open the door to his jeep and start to step in when he stops me.

"No, Jackie, I'm driving! You get in the passenger seat. I'm driving!" he demands, hastily pulling the keys from my hands and stepping in front of me. I am not as strong as him, so I submit and walk around to the passenger side.

Fighting to keep my composure, I sit silently in my seat, watching the car swerve in and out the yellow lanes. I look over to see if he's okay, he looks numb. He doesn't have a facial expression, but he notices me looking and he reaches over to grab my hand. He's never done that before, and I'm confused. *He's probably just sad and looking for comfort,* I think to myself.

After driving around aimlessly for about fifteen minutes, we pass a store where he stops and parks. I freeze.

"Let's go in and get something to drink," he says. I feel relieved we're not driving anymore and follow him into the store. He grabs a bottle of sprite, and we walk back out to the car.

Standing in the parking lot, I feel myself pushed against the car and turned around. His body is pushed up against mine, he starts kissing me.

"No!" I say with as much power as I could gather. I start shaking.

"Shut up! Just shut up!" he shouts, his hand over my mouth. I powerlessly try to fight back.

He opens the backseat door, picks me up, lays me down, and puts himself on top of me. My head is jammed in between the seat and the door. I feel stuck. I can't move. He takes off my pants, then my underwear. I am exposed. His body is heavy. I feel so small. I freeze.

It finally ends, and I burst into tears.

"Come to my house! Please!" he begs.

"No!" I yell back, grab my keys from his dash, run to my car (which was thankfully parked nearby) and drive home.

It's four in the morning as I walk into my house. I go upstairs and into my bathroom, take off my underwear, and stare at it as if it doesn't belong to me anymore. I throw it away. I stare down at my arms and legs and thought the same. My body isn't mine right now. *What just happened?*

Despite remembering falling asleep on the bathroom floor, I wake up on the couch downstairs. My phone rings. It's him.

I answer anxiously; he starts talking mindlessly, passively asking questions about irrelevant things. Unable to decide how to properly respond, whether I am supposed to be angry or scared or play dumb, I find myself stumbling over my words.

"Do you... uhm... Do you remember what happened last night?" my voice shakes as I finally manage to get my words to climb out of my chest.

"No way. Not at all. I blacked out and don't remember a thing. How much did I drink?"

I hang up, throw my back against the wall, and let my legs collapse to the floor. I feel like the only person in the whole entire world. I have never felt more alone, abandoned, isolated; like the life I once led was now over.

Sitting alone on the floor of my dad's office, I realize there is a choice in front of me that needs to be made. *Should I tell someone? If so, who? How am I going to cope with my pain?* If he really doesn't remember what he did to me, maybe it would be better to pretend nothing happened.

I get to work and try to act normal. My abuser has a shift tonight too, and I'm doing my best to avoid him. His section is far away from the host stand where I work, so I'm doing okay so far. I walk over to the bar to help run drinks, and I feel a familiar presence walk up behind me.

"Jackpot, what are you doing over here?" he asks as he jokingly pushes himself against me. I don't find it funny. I ignore him, pull myself back into composure and walk back to the host stand where I plan on staying for the rest of the night. I quickly realize that keeping this secret, pretending nothing happened, is not possible.

I go home that night and call my sister, planning on getting the words out to her in some way.

"Hey, Jackie," she answers, which surprised me because she rarely does.

"Hey. Uhm… "

"What's wrong?"

"Nothing! Uh, are you bringing a hair dryer on our vacation tomorrow?" I ask, unable to get the words out of what happened. She says yes, we get off the phone, and I send her a long text sharing the story of my assault that I couldn't manage to say out loud.

The one person I know I need to tell next was my abuser. If he actually doesn't remember, he needs to know. I text him, once more asking if he knows what he did. He says no. I ask him if he wants to know, and he says yes.

"Last night, you forced me to have sex with you," I say, uncomfortable using the word rape. He apologizes, tells me he feels terrible, and I feel confused. Am I supposed to forgive him? Is this supposed to be fixed now? Am I supposed to just move on with normal life now?

The next person I need to tell is my abuser's girlfriend, my best friend. There is no escaping that confession, no way that I can keep a smile over my face in our friendship without this secret eating me alive. The anxiety rippling endlessly through my soul might as well swallow me right up as I plan to make the call. How in the world am I supposed to tell her what had just happened? Telling her, my ride-or-die best friend, the Lizzie McGuire to my Miranda Sanchez, is going to put her in a place to have to make a choice between myself and the man she loves. I'm so afraid that she's not going to choose me.

I'm in Florida on what is supposed to be a vacation with my sister and aunt. I sit down on top of a dock, letting my feet dangle above the ocean. I hold my breath, dial her number, and somehow find courage within myself to put words to my trauma, without any certainty of how it would be received on the other end. Without even an ounce of confidence that I was worth being believed, chosen, loved in the middle of this. I spoke the truth, hung up the phone, and never heard the sound of her voice again. She chose him.

I find my own ways of coping alone. I lock my pain up tight, stuff it into a far back room in my body that I won't let anyone access including myself and leave it there as I go to party after party, drinking shot after shot. The observing world will believe I am okay, but inside my head, the Darkness is my dictator. If I'm not out getting drunk at a party filled with people I have mostly never met, waking up on random dirty couches and cold floors cluttered with red solo cups and half-empty bottles, I am alone in my room drowning in tears.

Word starts to spread about my assault, both at my work and outside of it. People respond in a variety of ways. Some stumble around the topic, making jokes to avoid any discomfort. Some pretend it didn't happen and smile as though everything was normal. Some condemn me, telling me it was my fault, telling me that I was victimizing myself. Or harassing me, telling me that I made it up or was probably drinking too much. Others can't even look me in the face. People that I hoped would protect me don't. People who I need to support me chose to shame me instead.

This had to have been my fault, I think to myself. *There is no other reason for these hollowing responses. I'm worthless. Garbage. Meaningless.* The Darkness grows louder in my soul--more dominant and relentless. It's monopolizing my entire life at a time when combating it with the truth is unheard of, especially since I don't even understand what the truth is.

There's no party to go to tonight, and my mom, who knows about my assault, has not talked to me about it.

"Don't tell your father," she tells my sister.

I walk inside my house. My dad is watching the game in the living room. My mom is making dinner. She smiles at me and asks about my day, but I ignore her and go upstairs to my room.

The stairs feel overwhelming, but I make it to my room. I slam the door behind me, crawl under my covers, close my eyes, and relive the night of my assault like grainy flashbacks of an old horror film. I can't get it out of my head. I feel powerless, vulnerable, broken. I wish I was dead. Nobody cares. The world would be better off without me. I wish I was dead.

I turn on an episode of Friends on my computer in bed and cry myself to sleep.

————

I woke up too early one morning in Boston. The sun had been setting fairly early, leaving it pitch black outside around 4 pm. It only makes sense that the days should seem shorter, but they didn't. My days have never, ever felt longer. To counter the length, I've been doing my best to try to sleep in as late as possible and go to bed early as well. But I keep failing.

Mornings have generally been the hardest, since they are the time when the whole day ahead of me is untouched. I'm so confused as to why I feel this way, why I can't seem to crawl out from beneath this dark cloud weighing down on top of me. I don't understand where this depression has come from. Not just depression, on the verge of suicide. Why here? Why now? I had to be making this up in my head.

I got myself out of bed, put on my jeans and jacket, and walked down the street to Tatte. It was loud in there, which made me anxious. I felt so sensitive to any little noise from the other customers, and the clanging of pots and pans in the kitchen didn't help either. I tried to ignore it by putting on my headphones and turning the music up, but it didn't help. I opened up a book to read but couldn't manage to concentrate.

The loud noises in the coffee shop grew to be too much, and my heart was pounding harder by the second. I looked down at my phone to check the time, hoping somehow the majority of the day was done. Turned out only about an hour had passed since I first sat down, and I had to get out of there.

I slammed my book shut, threw my things in my bag and walked back out into the cold. I couldn't stand the fact that I was alone, but I also couldn't fathom the idea of telling someone that I wasn't okay. If people knew, they'd feel burdened to talk about it. They'd want to get to the bottom of it, and I was too ashamed for conversations like that.

My phone started buzzing, I looked down to see my friend Megan's name on it. She had been calling me pretty often since I got to Boston, but I haven't been able to bring myself to answer. I did once in a while but made sure to only seem like I had enough time to have the surface level catch ups. She was someone who I knew would ask the hard questions and be able to notice if something was off, so I dodged her.

But I didn't want to be alone. Even if a conversation didn't go deep, I didn't care. I needed the presence of a human being who knew me. For the first time in a long, long time, I decided to call my mom. *Please pick up, please.* Waiting on her answer felt like I was waiting for a heart transplant. Walking the streets of Harvard Square, I saw friends walking with friends, families walking with families, everyone belonging with someone all around me. Finally, she answered.

"Awe, hi Jackie! What are you doing? I haven't heard from you in so long!"

Her voice reminded me of a version of myself I had lost touch with. It felt familiar. Freezing half to death, as usual in the northeast, I strolled around the streets of Boston, not having anything that I needed to do or places I wished to go. Distracting myself from the honesty silence has to offer, I took in my mom's voice for the first time in a long time.

Diligently listening through my headphones, taking every word captive, I imagined she was walking next to me. Her voice sounded like a memory I lost, one of who I knew I used to be. I closed my eyes and dreamt that she was there getting on the subway, walking through the grocery store, shivering from the bitter air outside on the icy sidewalks beside me.

Annoyingly familiar, yet somehow soothing, I listened to her lecture me through the phone about zipping up my coat to "protect myself from the elements." Or as I would be walking into a pharmacy, she would start panicking by the uncertainty of me not purchasing a spare tube of toothpaste and floss. This was the most I've ever loved listening to my mom nag me. I needed it. I actually hadn't flossed my teeth all month. Sorry, mom.

Before I knew it, the whole day had passed us by. Shopping, lunch, subway stops. Now there I was back where I started, at Tatte, still with my mom's voice talking through my headphones.

"I just wish you were here, Jackie! We could go to lunch, go to the movies, go shopping, whatever you'd want to do." I had to take my headphones out of my ears when she said that to hide my silent cry for help. I didn't want her to know. Nudging at my heart in ways she nor I knew it needed, this conversation stung.

I got off the phone with her, taking the sun finally setting as my confirmation to go back to my Airbnb and turn on a TV show to distract my mind for the rest of the night. The walk back felt longer than usual, and as soon as nobody was talking to me through my headphones, my chest tightened. It was dark outside now but looked even darker through my eyes. The cold air felt like knives stabbing me with every gust of wind.

I stepped inside my Airbnb, dropped my bag at the front door, and slid myself down onto the floor in the entryway.

"I am not okay," I whispered to myself.

I sat there for a moment and quickly realized that I couldn't take the freezing floor for a second longer, so I dragged myself into the living room and curled up on the couch under a blanket. I didn't have the energy to turn the TV on, so I just laid there and let the silence fill the room.

Tears rolled out of my eyes, which was the most honest part about me at that time. I felt as if I was all alone in the world. My phone buzzed again. It was Megan. I put it on the table and moved to the other side of the couch. *I am not okay.*

My heart beat incessantly, the only thoughts in my head telling me how worthless I was, how unloved, unaccepted, and broken. Nobody wanted me, and nobody wanted to hear the truth of how dark my head actually was. *Would anyone even believe me?*

I couldn't wrap my mind around the reality of how heavy the Darkness really was, nor could I give a name to it. How could someone like me possibly be *depressed*? I knew that I had battled with depression at seventeen, but back then it made sense. I had just experienced the most severe trauma of my life. Of course I was depressed! Of course I wanted to bury myself in parties and avoidance, but why *now*?

I had a great life, I thought. I just returned from the grandest of adventures. I had traveled through the most astonishing cities this country has to offer, living every night on the tip of my toes, singing along to songs sung by people who I believed to be legends. Now here I am in a new world where the cookies have yet to be tried, and the streets have yet to be explored. Why was I not okay? Why were the only thoughts that seemed to consistently control my mind about how much easier everything would be if I was dead?

I wanted a get out of jail free card. Maybe a car would hit me. Maybe the person next to me would have a gun. Maybe I would have some sort of fatal disease. I'd lay in bed, late at night, imagining how much easier everything would be if it all ended right now. I'd consider the future, even just as far as the next week, and feel completely powerless. I didn't want it. I didn't want to try anymore. I had already failed. I wanted out.

Day by day, I started to lose myself. Piece by piece. Moment by moment, I began to disappear.

VIII

I'm twenty-one years old. I'm lying face down in my living room in LA staring at a blank screen on my TV. My body feels too heavy to lift off of this couch. My world has been crumbling beneath my feet at every step I have taken for this past month. Although I was highly encouraged to take my shame to my death bed, I didn't listen. This month I made a decision to come clean about what has been happening with Steve, my boss and sister's ex-boyfriend, for the past year and a half. The moment my secret was exposed, I started losing every close friend I thought I had, and been written and read aloud letters condemning me, kicking me out of the church community group that I started. I can't move. I am disgusting, I hate myself, and I wish I was dead. I'm certain that I'm going to hell.

I can't live like this anymore. The one person I know I need to tell next is my sister, but I have no words to express how much that terrifies me. I wouldn't blame her for wanting me dead. I want that too. I wouldn't blame her for slapping me across the face, turning her back, and never speaking to me again. That's probably what I deserve. I can't take this secrecy for one second longer. I need to come clean. I need her to know.

"I need to talk to you about something serious," I text Alex. Now there's no going back, no getting out of this.

"Want to come over?" she responds, quicker than I expect.

I feel like I'm not a part of my body, like I'm watching myself get off the couch, grab my jacket and keys, and begin my journey to expose myself for the despicable human being I believe that I am.

I'm crying so hard that I can barely see through my windshield. The drive feels daunting in silence, so I turn on "Oceans" by Hillsong to drown it out.

"Please, God! Please help me! I can't do this!" I cry out as loud as I can as the song begins. The closer I get to her house, the faster my heart pounds.

I feel like I'm falling apart. Everything from the past is coming to the surface and I don't know how to control it anymore. I'm hurting people, I'm losing people, and it's barely even begun. I need to face my demons and come to terms with the choices that I've made. This is absolutely anything in the world but easy. I feel numb but like I'm breaking in half at the same time. How did it get this bad? I'm done waiting. I'm done avoiding.

My big sister is my hero. She has been for as long as I can remember. Losing her, even entertaining the idea of her hating me, the image of her eyes as her heart breaks because of *me*, I can't take that. That will be what kills me. But if I don't do this now, it will only get worse. Every time I hang out with her, my heart breaks more and more, piece by piece, grieving our relationship before it's destined to end. She thinks she loves me, but she doesn't know what I've done. She doesn't know what my shame is telling me about myself. But I can't hide anymore, I would rather the truth be known and leave me dead than wear this mask for one second longer.

I get off at the exit, make the sharp turn into her neighborhood, and pull over to the side of the road.

"I hate myself," I say out loud once more.

I stay parked for about twenty minutes to go through the lines of what I will tell her before running away. I open my mouth to rehearse but start to cry again. Practicing feels hopeless, so I start my car and keep driving until I reach her house.

I park, slowly climb out of my car and pace up her driveway. I hesitantly knock on the door. She opens it quickly and I see anxiety in her eyes. I have no idea what she thinks I'm going to tell her, but she looks scared. I break down in tears the instant I step inside her house, and she pulls me into her arms.

"You're gonna hate me forever," I say in between sniffles, unable to decide if I should push her away from me for her own sake or stay safe in her arms while I still can.

"I can never hate you, Jackie."

We sit down on the couch, staring awkwardly at each other face to face, and I can't feel my hands. I look down to see them shivering, but I still can't feel them. My body is going numb, all I have left to feel is my chest burning like hell.

"Do you want to tell me now?" she asks

"I can't. Can you just guess, please? I really can't," I beg.

"I don't know what to guess, Jackie, please just tell me?" Her voice grows more anxious and I realize I'm stuck. The words have got to come out.

I pull back my tears, look her in the eye, and I share my story. I tell her about her ex-boyfriend kissing me on tour and sleeping outside in shame. I tell her how I didn't stop him, how I chose to continue working for him, how sorry I was for lying and betraying her. I tell her how many more drunken mistakes there were after that, and how desperately I wished I had stopped it. I tell her how sorry I was and how I had never hated myself more in my entire life. I have nothing left to lose. She needs to know all of it, no details left behind. The words I thought I would take to my deathbed are now out in the open for all to hear.

Alex begins to cry, and I know what's coming next. I can't believe I just said all of these words out loud, I can't believe she knows the truth. She opens her mouth to speak and I cringe my body as if I'm preparing for a hit, waiting to be kicked out of her house forever.

"I love you, Jackie. I forgive you."

"What?"

"Jackie, I understand, I forgive you and I'm so happy you're talking to me about it. Of course I'm angry, but I'm angry at him! He's a thirty-one-year-old man, you were a vulnerable teenager!"

"But Alex-"

"We will work through our problems Jackie, but I love you and I forgive you and it's going to be okay."

Alex pulls me into her arms and holds me. This hug feels different than the first one. This hug feels different than every other hug she's given me over the past year and a half, and I think it's because she knows who she's hugging. She knows who I am, she knows what I've done, and she's still choosing to love me, to forgive me, to know me.

———

Running uncomfortably behind schedule, my friends and I pulled our bags through the Boston train station to catch our ride to New York City for Thanksgiving break. It was Kate, her other two best friends, and me meeting up with Kate's family there.

Thanksgiving in New York felt like someone else's dream, one that not one part of me felt like I fit the mold for. The shopping, the elegant winter coats, the five-course breakfast above the Macy's Thanksgiving Day Parade, the restaurants charging one hundred dollars a plate of miniature food. It was never a dream that crossed my mind when deciding on how to spend the holidays.

As we stepped onto the train and put our bags in their proper cubbies, I finally had a moment of silence to get my emotions straight. The Darkness took its normal course of clouding my head, but I did my best to hide it.

"You okay, Jackie?" my best friend asked.

"Yeah, I'm fine, just tired," I answered. *Tired* was my alibi.

The train arrived, and we made our way to the car that would take us to our hotel. I reached to open the door for myself, but the driver got out and beat me to it. Everyone is so excited to be here. I know I should be too, but all I can think of is how much I don't belong. *"Nobody actually wants you here,"* the Darkness was telling me.

Thanksgiving Day arrived, and I hoped I would be feeling better by then. The Darkness didn't allow that. I woke up early to get some quiet time in the hotel lobby and wrote down prayers in my journal begging God to take away my pain. I felt defeated and helpless on my own, but maybe by dinner, it would be just a memory and things would feel okay again.

It was dinner time now. We were all dressed in our holiday skirts and dresses, gathered around a round table at one of the nicest restaurants in NYC. That's what they tell me anyway but seeing the peculiarly small portions of food that are brought out, I'm not sure I would agree. They served lobster that I wasn't sure how to eat, so I just pretended not to want it and drank the ounce of soup they put in a tiny martini glass instead. Tiny soup, tiny glass- the pattern continued. I wasn't sure if I was supposed to drink it like a cup or use a spoon like a bowl, so I waited to see what everyone else did before taking my 50/50 chance of looking like a prestigious tiny food connoisseur.

Everyone continued in conversation through the dinner, talking about what they were thankful for and what they had learned in school that year. I didn't know what to say. I just wanted to get through the meal without running to the bathroom to cry. Every sentence or question that came to mind for me to say felt unnecessary and dumb, so I kept my mouth shut and kept myself looking occupied twirling my tiny spoon.

We finished our bite-sized pies for dessert and headed back to the hotel for the after-dinner walk. Everything was as normal. We were all linked arm in arm discussing our favorite foods and commenting on all the fancy clothing being shown in the windows when the Darkness arrived. I couldn't speak. I couldn't even maintain the fake smile I generally had when this happens. I don't think it had ever been this bad.

I didn't want to be alive. I didn't feel worthy of walking those streets and feared nobody wanted me there anyway. I felt isolated. I was the outsider, being tormented from the inside out, with no light at the end of the tunnel to offer me hope. I wanted to tell someone. I wanted so badly to be able to open up my heart and release these burdens that were suffocating me.

"What's going on? Are you okay, Jackie?" Kate asked as she noticed my sudden departure from the conversation.

"Yeah, yeah, I'm fine. I'm just kind of tired, that's all. I promise I'm okay," I stuttered as I instinctively tried to pull my cheeks up into a proper smile.

"Are you sure? Normally you comment on how pretty everything is," my friends teased, imitating the over-the-top enthusiasm that I generally share at the sight of a pretty brick building.

The next night, the walls caved in more rapidly. Some sort of internal alarm was going off in my brain, begging me to speak up, stop ignoring it, and get help. But I refused to listen. Gathered around another table in another restaurant, I couldn't even look my friends in the face. Conversation felt impossible, and I felt like I was going to throw up if I took even the smallest bite of food, even though this time it was normal sized. Kate announced earlier that she was mad at me but hasn't told me why yet, which makes sitting by her ridiculously awkward.

"Jackie, are you okay?" her mom asked.

"I'm okay, I'm just not really hungry," I responded as I moved the food around in circles on my plate, trying to make it look like I had eaten more than I did.

"No, you're not okay, what's wrong?" she asked again with urgency.

"Just, family stuff..." I whispered as an excuse but couldn't contain myself for one second longer. Right there sitting around the table, I burst into tears and excused myself to go to the bathroom.

"I'm so sorry," I mumbled as I quickly walked to the other side of the restaurant.

The bathroom was empty, but I hid in the stall anyway in case someone walked in. I sat down on the cold concrete floor, hugged my knees to my chest, and let myself feel freely. My crying was loud, desperate, and had a vengeance from being locked away for far too long. Suddenly, there was a knock on the bathroom stall.

"Jackie, I'm out here if you want to talk."

I opened up the stall door to see my best friend waiting for me by the sink, arms wide opened.

"Jackie, the reason I'm mad at you is because I know something is wrong and you're not telling me. You're my best friend. How am I supposed to be there for you if you don't tell me what's wrong? I know you and I know that you are not okay."

Was she serious? Was this my moment? I didn't feel ready to let her in. I barely knew how to explain it to myself. If I tried to say what was wrong out loud for another human to hear, I would sound insane.

"It's a lot. Can we talk more about it another time?"

"Yes, let's go back out there. I think everyone is waiting for us."

Kate gave me a hug, grabbed my arm, and walked me back outside to her family.

Thanksgiving break came and went, and we boarded our train back to Boston. It was a quiet train ride. Not much conversation was had. I stared down the aisle to see the other groups of friends rehashing their vacations, laughing at inside jokes, and falling asleep on each other's shoulders. I looked back to my friends, each reading their books to catch up for their classes, and I leaned my head back to try to sleep.

Waking up back in Boston the next morning, I had never been more aware of how much I needed help. Awake with the sun, the Darkness had still not left me alone. I wished I could fight back.

I was at a new all-women's gym seated on a bench press, listening to the song "All Will Be Well" when my phone buzzed. Glancing down to see what it was, a video was sent to me from a new friend, telling me how thankful she was that our lives crossed paths. Right there, right then, I started to cry. Thankfully there weren't any macho dudes to witness me all emotional next to my overly ambitious twenty-pound weights. Here was a friend who wanted to know me, wanted to care about me, but I wouldn't let her. I knew exactly what I was doing, and I was done with it.

With enough self-awareness to know that my moments of courage are often short-lived, I immediately texted Kate to tell her there was something serious that I needed to talk to her about. I was finally going to tell her what was wrong.

Watching the little typing bubbles dance around on the screen while waiting on her response was absolute torture. The anxiety in that is way too real. Now there was no way out.

What was I so scared about, anyway? Was it that whatever this mental illness was would declare me a crazy person? Too much to handle? Would it scare everyone away? Did it mean that I didn't know and love Jesus like I thought I did? I was filled with an unexplainable, shameful fear that I didn't know whether to believe or not.

After arranging a time to talk, I felt nauseous. Was I really about to open up about this? Was I really about to let my walls down this far and invite someone else into such a cold, confusing, scary piece about who I am? I had never spoken the things I was planning on saying out loud before. *Will she think I'm crazy? Will she even believe me?*

The coffee shop I chose to meet her at was by far the busiest in the city, especially at 11:30 am, which was when we conveniently planned on arriving. Yes, I'm talking about Tatte. I loved and hated that place for so many reasons. Like I've said before, if Instagram was a place, it would be Tatte. However, this wasn't exactly the prime spot to have this personal of a conversation. Not that I've been to every coffee shop in the world to be able to accurately compare, but I'm fairly certain I found the busiest one and this was it.

I pulled up, anxiously hunted down the nearest open pole to lock up my bike and maneuvered my body inside. She wasn't there yet, so I had time to remember how to breathe. I sat myself down on a stool facing the window, opened up my journal, and rehearsed what I planned on saying. *Breathe. You're going to get through this. She's going to understand.* I passed the long minutes waiting trying to convince myself I would survive this, unable to read what I wrote in my journal. My mind was racing too fast. A cold breeze swept in next to my stool as the door swung open. In walked a long blue winter coat, an uncertain smile, and a familiar face. There she was. I had no choice but to be ready now.

After a few minutes of small talk mixed with deciding which fancy French dish we wanted to share, I knew it was time to stop stalling. But as is typical for conversations this revealing, I froze up. Just imagine all of the word fumbling, lip biting, twiddling thumbs, packed like sardines' side-by-side with the other coffee lovers. As awkward as this conversation might be with five other people seated an inch away from our table, there we were. Could I *be* in a worse place to have this conversation?

I closed my eyes, somehow gathered up everything I knew I needed to say, all the burdens I was begging to be free from and put it all out there on the table for another human being to see. I told her about the Darkness, the prison of isolation I couldn't seem to crawl out of, and how often I thought about taking my own life. I told her why I wasn't eating, what I was afraid of happening if I did. I felt stuck. A silence that felt too long followed my confession. Then, finally, she responded.

"Jackie, you're my best friend. I want to walk through this with you. I want to be here for you through this. It's okay, I understand. I've experienced times like this too."

I stared at her blankly, unsure if this was real or not. It was a *too good to be true* moment that I could only remember happening in movies or on TV shows, but never in my own life. The thought of someone walking through this pain, this Darkness alongside me was like music to my soul. Maybe I didn't have to do this alone. Maybe I was going to survive, find real life again. *What took me so long to open up in this way? Why didn't I trust her with this sooner?*

exile

A few days had crept by since Kate and I sat in that little booth in Tatte. It had been less than a week since I found the boldness within my body to open up about my mental health, to let the real me be exposed. That conversation left me under the impression that the relationships in my life felt too good to be true. That there was a way out, a light at the end of my bitter, murky tunnel after all. I was going to be okay, I thought. I was not alone.

My hands shook uncontrollably--so violently that I hid them under the table, smothering them beneath the weight of my legs. I stared down at an untouched bowl of rice, which peered anxiously back at me, waiting for me to speak. My heart raced, my chest tightened, everything in my line of vision grew blurry.

"Jackie, sweetie, we need you to trust us. We love you. You're like a daughter to us," said Kate's parents sitting across the table. But nothing seemed to make sense at that moment. I didn't feel loved. I didn't feel like their daughter. Not anymore at least.

I had for the three years prior, but now I was an outsider.

The only words I could manage were "I'm sorry."

"Don't apologize! You don't have anything to apologize for."

If I didn't have anything to apologize for, why was I there? Why was I suddenly being told to leave? My blurry surroundings now started to spin. Other than *I'm sorry,* I had nothing else to say. I shoved my meal to the side and pulled my water cup close to take its place. I had been living in Boston for barely three months. Now I sat there, face to face with two people who had claimed me as family for the past three years, having strived with every piece of myself to find belonging and create a home in this city. I had dreams, visions, plans. I was constantly, from all sides, commended on the great job I was doing--by my best friend, my boss, my "family." I was a great employee, they said, and the best friend their daughter had ever had. But here, in the blink of an eye, everything I had been told was no longer relevant, and everything I held close was being stripped away. My job, my best friend, my "family", my home, my city. It was all gone.

I didn't want to be me anymore. I was so ashamed of how I'd, apparently, let them down.

"We need Boston to go back to the way it was before you were here," they told me.

I didn't want to exist anymore. Not once have I ever felt as exiled from my own personhood, own identity, own self.

I moved my gaze upwards, attempting to finally make eye contact with the two sitting across from me. Their arms once were open wide, their hearts once holding mine--but nothing would be the same from this day forward, that much was clear. Their voices started to disappear, fading off into the thickening air. Their lips were still moving, their eyes locked to mine, but I was left speechless and without clarity.

"I'm sorry..." I mumbled once more.

I sat still, unable to move as the conversation came to a close. They stood up, hugged me, held me upright and close to say their goodbyes. I held them tight, taking in their embrace one last time pretending nothing had changed. I laid my head on her shoulder, and let my tears pour onto her soft winter coat. Her hair smelled familiar, but her hug no longer felt safe.

She pushed me out from her arms and looked me in the eyes. "Trust us, sweetie, this is for you!"

As the pair began to walk away, one thing and one thing alone felt clear: the road for me in Boston had come to an end. *But where do I go from here?*

My body felt too weak to remain standing. As they walked out the door, I let myself curl back up into the metal seat. At last, I let the honest tears fall, tears that I had been choking back for the entirety of the morning. There they were. Loud, raw, naked, and real. The employees of the Chipotle I was in couldn't help but stare, not that I blamed them. I probably would have stared too.

There were two options in my head with what to do next. One felt torn into pieces, wishing to stay seated there forever and pretend this conversation never happened. Pretend I had never moved here, pretend everything was normal. Dissociating entirely from my reality. The other one screamed, "Get up! Get out! Go find a way to move forward." That part of my mind was a warrior, one who knew I was capable of picking myself up and stepping forward. But the warrior side, it was much quieter than I needed it to be. It was there, yes, but it needed an awakening. I couldn't take the tension for one second longer. I gathered the strength to stand up, threw my rice bowl in the garbage, and made my way out the door.

Emotionally paralyzed, I took my first steps as a new human being. One with an unexpected, disarming fresh start. The biting wind hit my numb cheeks, and I felt as if I had to learn how to walk again. I felt outside of my body, as if my soul was somewhere in the sky looking down at this broken person shuffling through the streets. Four more steps till I got to my locked up my bike that would take me back to my Airbnb. I could make it. I dropped my head down to watch my feet pass over the cobblestone roads that I had deeply admired every day I spent in this city. But Boston didn't belong to me anymore. These roads were no longer mine to admire. Ashamed to show my face to the other people wandering the streets, I reached my bike and quickly rode it back to pack my things and leave.

As I arrived, I locked up my bike and unlocked my front door. I stepped inside to discover that the air in my building was even more bitter than the air outside. I stood silent and still in the doorway, unintentionally holding my breath as I scanned the room for any sign of comfort. No pictures on the walls, no books on the shelf, no food in the kitchen belonged to me. Time was ticking before I had to catch my flight. I knew I had to pack, but what was *mine*? Even my *own* clothes and books felt borrowed.

My body was too weak to stand for one moment longer, so I sat down on a chair in the corner of the living room. Eyes fixed on the peeling glaucous wallpaper, panic overtook my body as I tried to make sense of why I was no longer welcome. Why the people who I had trusted more than anyone in the world, the people who claimed me as one of their own, were now sending me away to the other side of the country. My chest was caving in. I couldn't breathe. I felt like a prisoner locked up tight inside my own skin. I hated my skin. My heart was racing faster, faster, faster, head simultaneously pounding and spinning. Suddenly, my panic attack was interrupted by my buzzing phone on the floor. I looked down to see my big sister's name on the screen. I held my breath, gathered my sanity, and answered Alex.

"Hey, Jackie, what's going on?" she asked.

"Alex, I pretended Boston was perfect. I pretended everything was fine, but it wasn't. For the past three months of living here, I've been more deeply depressed than I have been in years. I've just wanted to be dead. Now I have two hours to catch my flight out of here. They told me I'm too much. They told me I can't be here anymore. I told them what I was going through and they're sending me away. I'm just supposed to leave and start over again?"

My knees gave out as I collapsed to the floor, desperately longing with everything I had to be rid of this depression, this Darkness camping out in my body. This housebreaker, this unwelcome guest—the Darkness had been demolishing the safety of my own self for far too long now.

"Okay, Jackie, breathe. I love you. It's going to be okay."

There was no part of me that could find truth in the words my sister spoke. *How in the world was this going to be okay? How in the world would I ever get to the other side of this?* Nothing could have convinced me of that much.

I forced myself to stop pacing, hung up the phone with Alex, took a deep breath in and booked my flight back to Nashville. I now had two hours left. Two hours left in this city, in this apartment, in this cold war I was fighting.

After stuffing whatever scraps I could find that belonged to me into my big red suitcase, I took one last look inside my Airbnb and made my way out the door.

PART TWO

lighthouse

I

"It's over. It's finally over," I muttered under my breath as I gathered my bags and stepped off of the plane. I was at last out of Boston, safely touching ground in Nashville without any intention of going back.

As I walked through the terminals to baggage claim, I felt like I was no longer watching my body go through the motions from above. I had stepped back inside my own skin. Dragging my red suitcases past the overly saturated country music postered hallways, I forced myself to be ready for my fresh start.

My friend showed up right on time to pick me up. I waved her down, threw what was left of my belongings into her trunk, and jumped in the front seat.

"Hey…"

"Well, hey! Are you okay?

"No…"

"Are you gonna tell me what's going on?"

"Not yet," I mumbled as I turned her radio up a bit and allowed my body to recline back into the seat. I turned my head to look out the window and held my breath for just a split second, as if that could make things suddenly feel whole again. As if, somehow in her car, I could find a way back to myself.

We pulled up to her house to find a few of our friends hanging out in the basement. It took me a minute to gather the courage to step out of the car. Once I showed my face back here, my failure and heartbreak would become evident. There would be no going back to the illusion I crafted so intentionally.

Less than 24 hours ago, my soul was vanishing in the east coast, genuinely feeling all alone in the world down in my rock bottom. Now, suddenly, that was over and I was here in this house with a crowd of people that claimed they loved me, but I had a hard time letting myself believe them. It didn't feel real.

Was I hallucinating? Was this a blessing? A punishment? I lost trust in my own feelings because every other hour I was in tears.

Hesitantly opening the door, I plopped my suitcases down in the middle of the floor and collapsed right on top of them. I was an awkward combination of giggles and tears, and nobody understood why.

"JACKIE! Wait, what are you doing here? How long are you in town for? I can't wait to hear all about Boston! It looks like you've been having such a great time!"

The right words wouldn't come out. Everyone seemed so hopeful for me, so excited to hear all the stories I would tell, the new and magnificent adventures I was heading out on next. I didn't want to disappoint anyone, much less paint a newly tainted picture of my life for them to see, so the words to an appropriate version of my story felt impossible.

"Oh, well, it's a long story. It's just so long, but Boston didn't work out. I'm here now though and I'm so excited to be back!" I claimed.

One by one our friends started to head home. I crawled upstairs, climbed into my friend's bed and let myself cry again. I normally waited to be alone for that, but given my current situation, that rule no longer applied.

"Is everything really going to be okay?"

"Yeah, I think it is, Jackie. You're home now."

The next morning, I woke up to an empty house. Everyone had left for work, as normal people do, and I was now in the midst of my first moment alone since leaving Boston. I stared at the ceiling, naturally wanting to get out of the quiet as quickly as I could, but something told me to stay put. Just for one moment longer, sit there, immersed in the discomfort, in the loneliness. I listened.

I made my way to my sister's house that afternoon and felt inextricably nervous. She was the first person I voiced my *real* story too, the first person I shared out loud what happened in Boston with, and now I was going to see her face to face. Lots of questions would be asked, and stories would be expected to be told. There was no illusion of myself I could present, no representative I could send in to convince her that I was great. The truth was out.

I pulled up to her house and sat in the car for a few extra minutes before going up to the front door. It was literally yesterday that I was vulnerable. Yesterday that I shared my most real, genuine self and got sent away to the other side of the country in response. That *really* happened, and now I'm trying again. If nothing else in this life makes me crazy, this does.

"Hi, Jackieeeeee!" Alex yelled as she pulled me in for a tight hug the moment I walked through the door.

"Hi..." I said back timidly, looking down to the ground. The instant I saw her eyes lock to mine, I immediately felt exposed. She held me for one second longer, then lead me outside to her back porch to talk.

Her house was warm. The kitchen was full, and the candles were lit. I looked down at my feet and noticed how slowly I was walking behind her. Every movement felt draining. I was exhausted, and something about being in my sister's home gave me permission to feel it.

"Okay, Jackie, start wherever you want. What happened? Are you okay?" I could tell she didn't know where to begin the conversation any more than I did.

I opened my mouth and instantly grew afraid of what words would come out of it. I loved my sister so much, there was nothing from our past that would prove her to be unsafe to share my hurts with. But what happened in Boston felt too real, too fresh. Suddenly every person I shared anything more vulnerable than what I wanted for dinner felt like a risk too great to take.

"It's okay. You can talk to me. What happened?" she asked, sensing my anxiety.

As soon as I started talking, I couldn't stop. The words to my story felt vindicating, freeing, groundbreaking. I told her about Boston, about how much I pleaded to make it through. I told her how pretty the cobblestone roads were, how frigid the wind felt, and how desperately I worked to create the illusion that I was on top of the world. I begged and pleaded to enjoy it there, yet somehow every night and day I still dreamed of killing myself. I told her about my friendship with Kate, how confused I was by what went wrong.

"We were like sisters," I told her. "I can't remember one fight, one disagreement, one conflict we ever had."

"I'm so, so sorry, Jackie."

"But, Alex, I've never in my whole life felt a heavier, scarier darkness in my mind than I did there."

"When did depression start for you?" She asked.

"When I was seventeen," I told her, "that's when I noticed it for the first time."

A few hours into the conversation, I began telling her about my eating disorder. That was a much newer, much clumsier conversation. But it needed to be had. All my cards were determined to be out on the table now. I told her how I stopped eating meals, how I was scared of gaining weight and losing people's love in return.

"Jackie, I love you. I hope you don't take this the wrong way, but I need you to know that I have *always* known these things about you."

"You have?"

"Yes! I'm your sister. Your *real* sister. Everyone tries to take you under their wing and be your make-believe *big sis,* but I really am. I know you. I always have. I'm here too. I've seen you grow up. We've gone our separate ways at times, but I still see you."

Hearing her speak these words brought me to more tears.

"This might sound weird, but *finally*, Jackie. I'm so happy that you're finally talking about these things. Now we can start to move forward. It's going to be okay. I promise."

Seven hours later, our conversation came to an end. Many tears were shed, but a different kind than before. These tears carried relief. I was far from healed, far from okay. But for the first time in a *long* time, I was on my way there.

Back at my friend's house that night, I laid glued to the couch. My body felt too heavy to sit up straight, and I was watching Parks and Rec reruns on the TV in an attempt to keep my emotions at bay. My phone began to ring. It was my friend Megan. I answered,

"I can't do this, Megan. I'm scared," I said to her on FaceTime, unable to hide my grief.

"What are you scared of, Jackie?" she asked, looking compassionately through the phone into my tired eyes.

"I, I just..." I stuttered. "I'm scared that I'm not wanted. I'm scared that I'm gonna break everything and hurt everyone somehow. I'm scared that everyone is better off without me,"

"Jackie, the girls and I in LA, we all love you so much. We're your best friends. Now get over here and let us love you!"

"Megan," I said in between sniffles, "I just want to crawl in a hole and sit there so that I can't hurt anything or anyone ever again. I'm too broken. Nobody should have to be around me."

"Jackie, if you sit in that hole, we're all just going to have to squeeze inside of it with you. We're going where you're going. We claim you."

There was a war in front of me, and every day presented a new battle to be fought. A battle for my mind, my heart, and my soul. Would I get up off of that couch and fight it? Or would I surrender, throw in my white flag and let the Darkness take my life as its prize? But what was once a one-man army fighting back was now gaining reinforcements. I was no longer fighting this war on my own.

I was back in LA now, sitting in my first of many necessary therapy sessions. Awkwardly attempting to cross my legs in a chair that was so big it might have swallowed me right up, I tried hard to focus my mind on the questions I was asked.

"Jackie, even your body language looks stressed. You look like you're trying to be proper and hold yourself together, but you're not okay. If this is going to work, I need you to show up. Not just physically, but show up emotionally," she said to me with a concerned look in her eyes. "Does that sound like something you can do?"

"Yes. I mean, I'll do my best," I stutter, trying to hide the fact that I just subtly uncrossed my legs to try to appear *less* tense.

I looked first at my keys placed on top of the stack of magazines, then one more time at the clock that I was hoping would move just a tiny bit faster.

Sitting on that stiff mustard yellow couch, I twiddled my thumbs to avoid eye contact. After two deep breaths in, I opened my mouth and found the words necessary to show up and bare my soul once again.

"The next choices you make in your life to nurture your mental health," she told me, "are vital."

II

Sitting in a new little booth in another cozy coffee shop immersed in the culture of LA, I sipped slowly on a freshly poured Ethiopian coffee that was a bit too hot to be enjoyed all at once. Walls dressed in old worn out brick, run-down wooden panels, and a whole lot of dreamers, this coffee shop was the perfect place for me to sit and think for a while. To be still and ponder the deepest of life's questions, reflecting on both the most arduous and life-giving of experiences from the past year, and wonder in deep anticipation about what this next chapter of my story will offer.

After taking in my pause, I realized that I needed to get a job. My job has been where I've found so much purpose in the past, it only makes sense that I would need one now to do the same.

Losing my job in Boston had affected me more than I was willing to admit. The persona I created to present to the world, the image of worthiness and purpose based on my job, it was gone. Now I'm left here with just me, my computer, and my tear-stained journals.

The music industry jobs that I had over the past four years; they looked and sounded a lot more glamorous than they actually were. I was comfortable there. I was content with the image of excitement my life had online, and the interested looks of admiration people gave me when they asked what I did for a living.

"Oh, I work in music... I'm on tour... I'm just about to leave to work a show for New Year's Eve on the other side of the country... I'm about to hop on a train to NYC for an event my artist is performing at this weekend. I'll get back to you," were some of the common answers I gladly offered when people wondered what I was doing with my life. There was a sense of dignity I held onto tightly, ignoring the fact that it was all a facade.

Now there I was in this new coffee shop in LA. I had no employer, no exciting upcoming tour, no merch to count. I sat and stared at the aspiring actors and writers and filmmakers swarming Los Angeles. I watched them live their passions, following the dreams that brought them to this big city. I tilted my head back, stared at the ceiling, and opened up a google doc on my computer. I had a story that I needed to tell.

I had originally begun writing my book *Finding Home* during my time in Boston. However, the version that I was writing then was a story drowning in avoidance. As I was living out my delusion of a perfect life on the east coast, I was writing pages after pages of a fictional story claiming to be a memoir. A book that would convince the world I had found my home, when I had honestly never been farther away.

When I initially began working on the project, I thought *finding home* meant moving to Boston. Now, six moves later, I am facing the obvious fact that I was undeniably wrong. I remember sitting tightly in my favorite booth at Tatte one blistery afternoon, I opened up that fresh new google doc on my computer and tried to make sense out of my turmoil and bring purpose to my life. *"If I could just find a way to communicate this in a story,"* I thought to myself, *"maybe, then, I'll be okay."*

With that intention, I wrote:

"How can a place like Harvard become home for a person like me? How could a place like Harvard feel like peace? Never, never ever in a million years did I even consider entertaining the idea of someone like me sitting in a school like that, nonetheless reside in the city of Boston. Never would I have pictured myself walking the halls in a dorm building of the crimson themed school, just trying to get down to the dining hall for this thing they called "brain break." Their brains must have been working pretty dang hard for a school to make something called brain break a nightly ritual. My brain didn't need a break as much as it just wanted the free sun butter and bananas they had down there. So, for me, it was a nightly ritual as well.

"According to the internet, there are over seventeen million volumes of books in all the Harvard libraries combined. Obviously, if it's on the internet, then it's true. That's a lot of books, you guys. What business do I have hanging out at a school holding seventeen million books? A school that is home to the world's next great leaders and doctors and all the things in between? There's even a small chunk of this book written from the most famous

library Harvard has to offer, Widener Library. People travel from all over the world to see that library. There's airport-like security at the front entrance. That's just weird."

That was supposed to be the first chapter of this book. That was supposed to represent my process of finding home, finding myself, and learning what my purpose is. I used humor, clever anecdotes, witty comments to disguise my emotions. Better yet, writing gave me a sense of pride. The idea of introducing myself as an author, or even just in the process of writing a book, gave me more self-worth than I had before. But none of it was real.

I had to make something out of this. I had to bring purpose to this story. The cold hard truth of what happened. The honest tears that were shed. They have meaning and beauty and they deserve a place to be shared. That day in LA amongst the aspiring filmmakers, actors, dreamers, I decided to join in. I decided to try again, to dream again. But this time it would be different. This time, it would be real.

Every morning from that day forward I would wake up, drink coffee, and sit myself down in a cafe to put my story onto paper. Not the pretty version. Not the glamorous "Rockstar lifestyle" tale that I had told before. It was time for the honest, gut-wrenching reality. Page after page, draft after draft, I was determined to let my voice be heard.

I tried to be honest with myself, honest in the chapters and the pages. But I was terrified. These people that hurt me; they were family. They were on my side before. Now here I am, desperate to feel free from this burden that I've been carrying. But if I share, what will they say? I felt responsible to defend everyone who had hurt me, to make excuses for them, to make myself the villain of my own story.

Every day, I wrote out my process. I carefully tiptoed around the lines that I was afraid to cross, attempting once again to create an edited purpose-filled image with where I was at and what had happened to me. I tried so hard to create a nice moral and lesson-learned at the end of each chapter, of which I hadn't actually experienced yet.

At about a hundred and fifty pages in, five months later, I thought I was done. I announced my completed project to my friends proudly, looking at the excitement in their eyes as I claimed the worth that my finished book brought to my life.

"Hey, will you read my book and tell me if you think it's good or not before I send it out to get published?" I asked my friend Megan one night.

"Yeah, of course! Send it over and I'll read it as soon as I can."

About a week had gone by since I sent my book to Megan, and I had yet to hear any thoughts. I felt so vulnerable. I looked down at my phone to see a text from her telling me that she wants to call me to talk. I nervously agreed, plugged my phone into the speakers in my car and waited for her to pick up.

"Finally!" I thought to myself.

After a few minutes of small talk, I could tell there was something she was nervous to tell me.

"Megan, what's going on? Did you not like it? Was it okay?" I asked anxiously, feeling like my whole identity was on the line.

"Jax, asking me if your book is good is a hard question to answer. I read it, and I loved it because I love you and I know you and your story. I know what you have been through this year, but Jax..."

"Oh no," I thought to myself, "this doesn't sound good."

"It's just not ready yet, Jax…"

I pulled over, parked my car, sat down on the ground, and hugged my knees tight to my chest. This book was my world, my worth, all I have worked on every single day for the past five months. It was my therapy, my story, my purpose. I poured my heart and soul into this and hearing my friend's words broke my heart.

"Jackie, it's good. The story is good, but it's just not done yet. You're too close to it. You haven't given yourself time to heal yet, time to really soak in the story. It's only been five months since you left, Jax…"

"But Megan, it *has* to be done. I have a deadline. I gave myself one. I worked so hard on it, it's all that I have." I begged as I tried to hold back my tears.

"Jackie, get the deadline out of your head. Let yourself sit with this story, let yourself re-enter. It's going to be okay. It's just not done yet."

"Can I just give it one more month? One more month to re-look at it all?"

"No deadlines."

"But Meg-"

"No."

I sat on that sidewalk, I cried into the phone, and my chest grew tight. How did I end up here? How am I still not good enough? What do I have to present to the world now, to show that I belong? To show that I am worthy?

"Jackie, you are bigger than this book. Your life is bigger than this project. Your career does not define you. Give yourself time, space, anything you need to really heal without the pressure of finding a moral at the end. Go outside, go jump in the ocean, longboard down the beach, anything to remember who you are apart from writing this book."

She was right and I knew it. I hated that she was right.

"Love you, bud. We'll talk soon," she said as we got off the phone.

"I want to love myself. I want to see who I am underneath what I do, what I sell, what I write," I said out loud in my car ride home. "This is my moment. I am still worthy."

III

I was lying in bed one night, watching the raindrops hit against my window. I was tired, physically and mentally, so I decided to take a night in to read a book in bed.

I rolled over to the bookshelf beside me, scanned it up and down to pick out my date for the night. A thick, quarter-of-the-way-finished Russian novel from my time at Harvard was taking up a big chunk of space on the shelf, leaving me feeling a tad guilty for *still* not being done with it. I honestly thought I had lost that book in the move, and was relieved, to say the least. Anna Karenina was the name, and for a large portion of my time in Boston, I had battled through the pages of that book as quickly and diligently as I could, trying my best to keep up with my friends studying it in their classes.

There were so many characters, each one referred to by a million different names. How was I supposed to keep all of them straight when I have enough other people in my real life to remember?

"Vronsky," I began to read out loud, and immediately had to put down the book to google which character he was again. Pulling out my laptop and making my way to the internet, it hit me.

"Why am I *still* trying to read this book? Who the hell am I trying to impress now? What the hell am I trying to learn?" I asked myself, a bit too loudly. But loud was necessary.

I slammed the book shut, threw it to the other side of the room, and pulled out my old Harry Potter book instead to accompany me for the night. I opened the cover and felt a vaguely familiar magic in the words on the page, an invitation to a story that I needed to be a part of. There were no words to google, no characters to mix up, just a beautiful story about friendship and magic and everything that my soul needed.

"Hey, Jackie," I heard after a few knocks on my door.

"What's up?"

"Turner is here if you want to come hang out! We're just going to have some wine and hang out in the hot tub," my friend Faith asked. I finished my chapter, carefully folded the page over so I could

164

return to the magic later and crawled out of bed to go join my friends.

"Hey, Turner, how's it going?" I asked joyfully as I walked into the kitchen.

"Hey, Jackie! It's great to see you," Turner said as she stood up to give me a hug. Turner is the type of person who knows what she thinks, who she is, and is not afraid to make that known. She's confident and bold, yet extremely empathetic, compassionate and kind.

"It's great to see you, too! Mind if I join you guys?" I ask as I pour myself a glass of wine.

"Of course! How's it been staying here in Nashville?"

"It's been good. I've actually been learning a lot about myself while I've been here."

"Really, like what?"

I opened my mouth to respond, then quickly realized how afraid I was to let anyone know what I had going through my head. I normally didn't voice controversy, and I normally didn't share what I was thinking unless I had it all prepared and thought out before it left my mouth.

This had been a huge year for me, and a lot of my opinions that I had before were changing. Opinions about my faith, my sexuality, my relationships, politics, you name it. But speaking my opinions has never been a strong suit of mine.

"Well, lots," I felt myself start to become a bit heated, needing to get some things off my chest that I hadn't said out loud before.

"Like what? You can talk to us about whatever you want.

I began to speak up, but I remembered how people don't like it when I get mad. People like me as the happy, sweet girl that asks good questions and doesn't cause any tension.

"I just am learning that I have a lot of opinions about a lot of things…"

"Jackie," Turner said with a soft smile, "your opinions are very welcome here."

No one had ever said that to me so straightforward before. Not that I had been in too many conversations that would have led to that confirmation being needed, but hearing Turner tell me that my voice mattered, that my opinions were welcomed and accepted in this space, even if they didn't match up to hers or anyone else's for that matter, my opinions were mine. My opinions mattered.

I looked her in the eye, couldn't help but smile the pure kind of smile, not the forced kind, and breathe a sigh of relief.

"Well, alright. I'll tell you all about it!" I announced after taking a sip of wine.

And that I did. I spoke what was on my heart, my mind, and my spirit without concerning myself with being agreed with. I didn't filter out what might not be okay. I didn't adjust my opinions to be popular or to match theirs. I didn't try to use big words to sound smarter than I was, I just spoke. I spoke like I had nothing to lose, and only more of myself to gain.

A few weeks later, I was having dinner with a friend. This is one that I hadn't seen in a while and one that used to intimidate the hell out of me when it came to confrontation of any sort. She had her strong opinions, and in the past, I had tended to keep my mouth shut if there was a disagreement. She was older than me, and I never felt capable of being smart enough to have an opinion worthy to say to her in conflict.

"So, Jackie, I don't know how you feel about this whole *gay* thing," she said hesitantly. The reason this came up in conversation now, and had multiple other times throughout the year, was because my sister got married to a woman. She married her best friend, and all of my friends felt the need to share their opinions with me about it. I wasn't surprised when most of the opinions entailed how wrong it was.

"What about it?" I asked nervously.

"Well, I don't know how you feel, but I just feel that it's wrong. Marriage is between a man and a woman. God said so. Don't you think God put laws in place for a reason? Are you afraid for her?"

I looked out the window, completely overcome by anger. She knew how I felt. I had already told her before earlier this year. Was she pretending to forget? Was she pretending I didn't feel that way? I took a deep breath in, went through the different possible outcomes of this conversation in my mind, knew damn well what my opinion was, and decided to speak up.

"No, I'm not scared for her."

"You're not?"

"No, because I don't think it's wrong. I understand that you do, and that's okay, but I'm in a different place. I have a different opinion. I've done a lot of research. I've studied a lot of the old Hebrew and Greek from verses a lot of Christians use against it, and I just don't think it's wrong. I think it's beautiful. You don't have to agree with me, but that's just how I feel."

I swallowed hard, not sure if I sounded as confident as I tried to, or if my fear of sounding stupid and causing tension showed through my voice.

"Oh, well, okay."

I turned to look back out the window, and I couldn't help but smile. I was proud of myself. I felt smart, capable, unapologetic. I wasn't trying to impress, nor was I googling words on my phone to sound wise. I spoke from my heart, and that was enough.

"Jackie, what would you think and believe if there were no other voices in your head?" she asked.

"What do you mean?"

"You used to think for yourself, Jackie. You used to have your own opinions. I spent so much time teaching you about the Bible, and I don't want to preach at you, but I'm so worried that you're just trying to get your sister's approval again. I'm worried that you're not thinking for yourself. So, I want to know what you would think and believe if there were no other voices in your head?" I could feel my blood begin to boil.

"I know what it feels like to keep my mouth shut when people are saying things that I disagree with. I know what it feels like to blend in and go with the flow out of fear of confrontation. I know what it feels like to not have my own opinion, but to hold onto someone else's instead. But now, now I know what it feels like to not do that. To think for myself. This is it. This is how I feel, and I know that you disagree with my opinions. But I'm okay with that. This is how I feel, and I'm not backing down."

IV

Butt glued awkwardly on top of the stiff metal chair, immersed amongst the busy health-conscious shoppers of the Whole Foods Market I wandered into this afternoon, eyes staring downward at my boxed-up lunch, I felt like a failure. *"I can't do it. I can't eat this. I have to leave,"* I thought to myself, looking around to make sure no one was watching. After one more glance at the towering salad I had initially intended on eating for lunch, I stood up, tossed the box in the trash, and made my way out. *"This is never going to change…"*

On the walk of shame back to my car that afternoon after trashing the overpriced salad I was hoping to eat, I made a different decision than I had in the past. I phoned a friend.

"Hey bud, what's up?" Megan said enthusiastically as she answered the phone. For the majority of the year past, she was the one who called me when I wasn't okay. She called, I ignored, and proceeded to pretend things were wonderful. This time, patterns changed.

"Hey, so… I haven't eaten a meal in five days. I just felt like I was supposed to tell you," I said nervously, still parked inside the Whole Foods parking garage.

"Hey, I love you. You know that?" she responded. I felt awkward, exposed, naked. I didn't use to tell people this. I didn't use to let anyone know what was happening in my head here. But my therapist's words echoed in my mind that day walking out of Whole Foods.

"The next steps you take regarding your mental health, Jackie, are vital. It's life or death right now."

I hated calling Megan that day. I dreaded the accountability to make the change that would bring me into health. I didn't want someone actually making me eat a meal, monitoring my diet, knowing the nitty gritty details to how I felt about my own body.

"You have to *truly* want the life that comes after the awkward conversations. There's no faking your way through this," my therapist told me.

Megan and I talked for a while. I stumbled around my words, but at least I had words. I'm sure I didn't make sense, but I was trying. That was what made all the difference. I had to start somewhere, no matter how clumsy it felt.

The way I imagined myself in a conversation like this was knowing exactly what I wanted to say, exactly what was wrong, completed with a good moral learned at the end to communicate my resilience. Without the cleaned up redemptive ending, I wouldn't dream of sharing. Lately, I've been learning that that is not the point. I can't just isolate and deal with my problems alone until I have a picture-perfect flowing moral to present to the world at the end. Someone needs to be let into the mess before it's cleaned up and organized. I have to let someone hear the stumbling and the uncertainty and offer not only another voice of insight, but more importantly a voice of love. I have fears, and even before I overcome them, people need to know. That's where the connection is. From my experience, I have found that healing comes a lot faster when you let trusted people into the brokenness alongside you.

A few days later, I was in another counseling session opening up about the same conversation. She was asking me the same kinds of questions my friend was but in a bit more of an intrusive fashion.

"Jackie, look at me," my therapist instructed.

"I'm trying, I promise," I said to her in between the breaths I used to keep myself from crying.

"What lie are you believing? What do you think you're gaining by being skinny?"

"I think," this was it, there was no hiding now, "if I can be thin enough..."

"Finish the sentence Jackie, you can do it," my therapist said handing me a tissue as I failed in my effort to choke back more tears.

"If I can be thin enough, I would be worthy of love. I'm afraid of people not loving me."

"When I was 19," I told her, "I was living in a distorted relationship with a guy that one day thought I was the dream, and the next wanted nothing to do with me. This lasted for about a year and a half. He wouldn't stop talking about how good I looked thin, how I "used to be thicker" but now I was thin, so I looked great. In order for there to be more days where he did want something to do with me rather than not, I needed to get my body image down perfect," I told my therapist.

"But this was three years ago," she said, "If he's not a current voice of influence in your life anymore, wouldn't you just be all better now and not care?"

"Well, I guess? What do you mean?" I asked nervously as I clenched the arms of my chair, looking at the clock to see how many minutes left until we were done.

"There's something more here, Jackie. We'll get to the root. One step at a time."

At that moment the truth became a bit more evident than it had been before. I believe, through both my experiences growing up and in the dysfunctional relationship with Steve, I subconsciously tied being thin to being loved. My eating disorder developed as a side effect of my fear of rejection. Rejection stings.

"But what would happen if I wasn't living in that fear? What would happen if it didn't matter to me what people thought?" I thought to myself.

My counselor introduced me that day to something called an "eating disorder voice" and a "healthy voice." Whenever I have those thoughts about not eating a meal because it'll make me unlovable, that's my eating disorder voice talking. My ex-boss, Steve, had given the original language to the eating disorder voice in my life. In opposition, a healthy voice would tell me that feeding my body nourishing food is loving myself well. It's what I need to thrive, grow, and dream. It's a primary part of being a human being. To get healthy, I needed to start practicing replacing the eating disorder voice's truth with that real truth instead.

In this uncomfortably revealing session, my counselor asked me to do this little role-playing game. I was supposed to play the part of the eating disorder voice, and she was going to be the healthy voice. I was up first.

"You can't eat anything. You have to only drink green juice so that you can be skinny," I said avoiding eye contact, as embarrassed and red as I have ever looked in my life.

"No, you need to eat real food to nourish your body so that you'll have the energy that you need to get things done today. You need the energy to write books and run outside, and everything else you like to do," she combatted as the healthy voice.

"But if you eat, you won't be skinny and people won't like you as much," the eating disorder voice fought back. This was mortifying.

"No, Jackie. If you don't eat, then you're going to get depressed and not want to hang out with anyone. You're just going to be isolated and alone." The isolated and alone statement; that's what got me.

I was at my friend's house setting up for a birthday party in the middle of a pretty rocky week after that infamous counseling session. Cutting up snowflakes and taping blue balloons to every square inch of banister we could find, one of my friends was cooking himself some dinner. He was making a sweet potato and salmon, and boy did it look good. All I had eaten that day was a banana, hoping to make it through the end of this party without snacking too much on chips and dip.

Pulling his meal out of the oven, we sat across from one another as he ate his fish and I told him about some random story I thought he might find entertaining. He was kind yet came off a bit shy for the majority of the night before this moment. Wiping his face with a napkin after his last bite of salmon, he vibrantly leaped out of his shell as if he had become a whole new person. Dancing up out of his seat, he started parading around the house not caring in the slightest bit who thought what. I didn't know what to do. I didn't know what was happening, so I just giggled a little and continued putting up balloons.

"You ate some food, didn't you?" his roommate asked jokingly as she walked into the room.

"Oh, yeah. You know how I get when I eat a good meal! I'm a whole new person!"

I sat there, smiling and speechless, like a piece of me received a layer of healing I didn't expect to find.

Food is not the enemy of friendship and togetherness. It's the opposite. That might sound silly, but when something is ingrained in your mind as truth for so long, learning that it's not is an eye-opening experience.

Somewhere in my story, I got it stuck in my head that to experience friendship, acceptance, and love, my body has to look a certain way. That certain way revolved around being skinny, and I thought the way to achieve that goal was to not eat. Desiring that love, friendship, and belonging is not wrong. It's natural. But the deceptive way I tried to get it, that was a fundamental cause of the unhealthy relationship I had with food.

You know that vindicating feeling you get, just for a moment, when you get out of an unhealthy relationship that you were so intimate in, then see that person and the truth of who they are makes a little bit more sense than it did before? Reflecting back on the dysfunctional relationship that originally planted this eating disorder voice into my life, that's how I felt. It sure did feel free.

I'm not claiming to be all healed. I'm smarter than that now. I know that this is all a process, one that will take time, and one victory doesn't mean I've reached the finish line. Instead, this is me wanting to celebrate this small victory because I believe it matters, and in a way, I believe it will bring someone out there hope. Hope is worth it.

It has become obvious to me that there won't be healing in this area outside of relationships. I have to talk about this. I have to open up. I have to let people see this side of me instead of living life smiling on the outside while building this secret eating disorder empire under the ground. I believe that's why it lived for so long, even after Steve was out of the picture. I wasn't letting relationships heal me.

Relationships can mend and heal nearly anything. We need each other's sacred souls to feel alive, to embrace what it truly means to be human. I'm talking about the kind of relationship that loves you, celebrates you, believes in you, speaks life into you. Those are the kind of people I want in my life. Those are the kind of friends that can heal me just by being present. Having someone to remind me that sometimes life is messy. It's tiring and intimidating, but we need to be reminded that we're not crazy from time to time. Even if having people around you is just for the sake of another living breathing soul in your life that shows you that it's not just you, that can save a life. That matters.

———

It's been about a year since first stepping off the plane that took me from Boston to Nashville. It's, again, pouring rain outside as I'm driving my car aimlessly around town. I pulled over to a yoga studio, parked my car and walked inside.

"We're in room 1," the lady at the front desk said as I walked up. "Go in whenever you're ready, Jackie!"

I grabbed a mat, walked into the locker room and sat down on the bench. I slipped off my shoes, my socks, and my jacket. I put them in a cubby and almost walked out to the studio, but I stopped. I turned around and took off my shirt as well. I was now only wearing a sports bra and my leggings, just like everyone else. I was exposed, but I felt okay.

I walked into the studio and saw my safe spot in the back corner. The mirror was there again, and I remembered I was supposed to avoid it. I remembered I'm not supposed to see my reflection, so I spread out my mat in my corner behind another girl to hide me from myself. I laid down on the floor, closed my eyes, and breathed deeply in.

The teacher came in and turned on the music as she asked us to stand up in mountain pose. We were again, instructed to keep our eyes closed, and I was relieved.

"Okay, class. Whenever you're ready, open your eyes."

I opened my eyes hesitantly, clearly remembering how this made me feel the last time I was here. But I felt brave for some reason. I felt different. I moved my mat to the side, out from behind the lady I was planning to hide behind, and I looked myself up and down in the mirror. There I was, still there, still me. I looked at my legs, my stomach, my arms, and shoulders. I saw my eyes. They looked tired, but not broken. I saw power in them.

I then caught a glimpse of another girl's reflection across the room. She's thinner than me, more toned and confident, the way I felt like I was supposed to look. I looked back at myself and the power in my eyes had gone.

"Okay, class. Now go down on your mat into a child's pose and close your eyes once more."

I bent down and rested my face on my forearms. I was angry now, upset that I was stuck here still. Slowly, I opened my mouth. The room was silent, people would hear me if I spoke, but I felt as if I didn't have a choice.

"I want to love myself," I whispered. "I want to love my body."

I opened my eyes to glance around. People must have heard me, but I didn't care.

"I love myself!" I said even louder, "I love who I am. I am beautiful. My body is mine and I love it! I want to love it better!" I was sure people heard me this time, and I became embarrassed and went back to a whisper.

We stood back up into mountain pose and I opened my eyes once more. The same girl was staring back at me in the mirror, and my body looked just as it did before. But this time I saw power come back into my eyes. Strength and dignity, too. They looked full, empowered, brave. I moved my stare from my eyes to my torso, it looked different than it did before. I saw my legs. They looked different too. I breathed in deep, slowly, and felt as if my exhale spread life into this room.

I closed my eyes and whispered again softly, "I love myself. I love my body. I love who I am."

The class was ending, and I was filled with gratitude. The teacher sat down and put her hands in prayer position.

"The light in me sees and honors the light in each of you," she said and bowed.

I picked up my mat, walked to the locker room and put on my shoes and jacket. I walked out the door to my car and paused to see my reflection in the window. I didn't hide.

"I love me."

V

Ever since I was that bubbly little girl spinning around freely in her pink nightgown, I have been head over heels obsessed with animals. Dogs, dolphins, hippos, wolves, you name it and I guarantee you that I was infatuated with it at one point in my life. When I was in elementary school, my childhood best friend Maddi and I used to sit in the animal section of the media center, oohing and awing over photos and books of the different dog breeds we found. We would study our brains out on them as if our nine-year-old careers depended on it, determined to become experts someday.

We took this so seriously that we even voluntarily stayed inside from recess to get in extra study time. We planned on putting together research projects on the different dog breeds we were becoming experts on and hoped to treat our fourth-grade class to a presentation of all the wonderfully interesting things we had learned. Because, obviously, what else do a bunch of nine-year-old kids want to spend their time doing? Maddi and I were canine connoisseurs, they should be grateful for a chance to see our presentation.

I had desperately wanted a puppy of my own for way too long. When I was about fourteen years old, I schemed a whole plan with my friend Sehler to trick my parents into letting me have one. My dad told me that the only way I could have a German Shepherd, the dog of my dreams, was if I found one on the street. Ah-ha! Let the scheming commence.

Sehler and I worked night and day searching everywhere we could find for a little puppy I could afford with my weed-pulling money. We looked in all the shelters, contacted breeders, pet stores, the whole nine yards. Our plan was to buy a puppy, bring him home, and oh so cleverly convince my parents that I had found him on the street. We would then post up "found puppy" flyers around the neighborhood, and unless some other kid was also scheming to get a puppy, it would have played out flawlessly. Unfortunately, the plan failed miserably. I was caught and continued to remain puppy-less.

In the middle of my life's chaos post-Boston, my therapist recommended something that was music to my ears: a therapy dog. Who knew my depression could make my fourteen-year-old dreams come true! I obviously didn't think twice about the suggestion, (literally) jumped into my car right after the session ended and sped to every animal shelter in the Los Angeles area. Trust me, that was a lot of shelters. But none held my puppy, so I took to Craigslist where I met the dog of my dreams, Phoebe.

I was told to meet the puppy salesman in an empty lot across the street from his house. I had never purchased a dog before, so I guess this seemed fairly normal. He pulled up in a tinted black car, got out to shake my hand (his hand felt like a dead fish), silently opened the back door and pulled out a kennel with two puppies squeezed inside.

He opened the kennel to let out the two cutest, dirtiest, smelliest golden retriever puppies I had ever seen. Their cuteness obviously distracted me from their smells, so I knelt down in the parking lot and found true love at last.

"I'll take her!" I yell after about thirty seconds of snuggling this muddy pawed puppy.

"Okay. She's yours," he said as he grabbed my money and got back in his car to drive away.

Was this a sketchy situation? Probably. Do most puppy transactions happen in an empty parking lot? Who knows? My tunnel vision only saw the adorable fluff ball in need of some love, so I figured the rest was a problem for future Jackie.

My intention of getting this puppy, I should add, was to take care of my mental health. I was told that having something cute to take care of would be good for my depression. I loved being needed. I loved having a purpose outside of myself, so I didn't doubt that caring for this little one would bring me some joy.

We got home late that night. I snuck Phoebe inside (my apartment had a no pets policy, but apparently my tunnel vision excluded that as well during the transaction) and she made herself right at home. Leaping and yelping, Phoebe explored her new-found freedom as if it was the first time she had been allowed outside of a two by four kennel (which was honestly not unlikely). I picked her up, cradled her in my arms, and panicked. In her neck, there was a lump.

My mind jumped to the worst possible con-clusions, and I broke down in tears.

"I killed her! She's gonna die! What am I gonna do?!"

I laid on my floor, unsure of how to care for myself through an extreme anxiety attack while this puppy might be dying right in front of me. I looked up the vet that her seller claimed to have gotten her shots from and found that it was a one-star rated clinic in Iowa. *What the hell is happening?*

I then proceeded to text the Craigslist guy, who of course didn't respond. I went to pull up the ad he placed, which of course he took down. I was screwed.

I brought my sick puppy to the vet the next day where I found out all of the worst case scenarios I was losing sleep over were wrong. I was then handed a bill much larger than I had anticipated. I was now preparing in my mind to live on the street. I was going to starve. I was going to sleep in a tent. I was going to make a sign asking specifically for Justin's Maple Almond Butter and bananas so I wouldn't starve. At least I could use my puppy to get some sympathy from the local pedestrians.

A couple days went by and I continued my downward spiral. *Isn't being needed supposed to help me?* I mean, I was most definitely needed. My therapist was right about that. But in the middle of being so needed, I wasn't sleeping, wasn't eating, and now living in an anxiety attack as my new normal.

I had never cleaned up more poop in my entire life. I swear to you, I am not exaggerating. I would put this puppy in her kennel for ten minutes- TEN MINUTES- and I would come back to her covered in her own poop. Every. Single. Time. She's lucky she was cute, because I had never been so close to pure hatred in my life.

This dog needed me. I was well aware of that. I knew that was the point, but goodness gracious I had never given so much of myself in my life and I forgot that I needed myself too. I was drowning in my own tears, constantly on my hands and knees cleaning up dog poo and hadn't eaten a meal since I left that sketchy abandoned parking lot where all of this began.

I have come to find that a common theme in my search for belonging is needing to be needed. From the way too many days I worked as a personal assistant (more like a glorified adult nanny if you will), I was used to my world revolving around some-one else's. I was used to dropping everything to bring my boss a cup of coffee or skip my own dinner plans to do a last-minute photo shoot so he could have a new glamour shot to post on Instagram. It felt like a routine to say no to myself so that I could be "on call" in case I'm needed to cook someone a meal or do someone else's laundry. The saddest part of all this was that for all this time, I felt like that was why I was wanted around. If I didn't have anything to offer. I had no place at the table. If I didn't have a job to do, I didn't belong. Those calls to do laundry and cook meals and bring people coffee, they gave me a dangerously false sense of purpose.

I've found that I can't for the life of me seem to go support my friends playing a show somewhere without offering to take their photos, film their sets, or sell their merch. I feel like in order to be welcome there, I need to be helping in some way. Sometimes this is out of genuine kindness, but other times I'm starting to notice that it stems from a fear of not being needed.

"If there's nothing I can offer, if there's no way for me to help, what is the point? Am I even wanted if I have nothing to offer?"

I need a job to do. I need a person to help, or in this case, a puppy to clean up after. I need to be making someone else happy or I'm afraid I have no purpose, no belonging, no reason to be around.

And what's even worse than not having a job to do, is failing to do the job well when asked. Failing to comfort my friend who lost her baby back when I was 17. Having no words to say to soften the pain brought me excruciating self-loathing. Not being able to help my best friend in Boston after her dog died, not having the appropriate words to say then did the same thing. Now there I was with a puppy that literally needed me for survival, and I couldn't even do that. *I need me first.*

About a week after this puppy transaction in the parking lot, I decided to give myself permission to throw in the towel. I called around and found Phoebe a nice giant mansion in Malibu to move into. So just for the record, if anyone out there reading this book thinks that I am heartless for giving away a baby golden retriever, just know that she's pretty well off. Phoebe is doing better than all of us. She went from the literal bottom to hanging out in her new crib next to the Getty Villas. She's fine.

After dropping her off, I was absolutely devastated. I had never felt more like a failure in my whole entire life. That puppy needed me, but I couldn't do it. I couldn't take care of her, and I had never felt more purposeless in my life.

I left Phoebe's new mansion and went to lay on the beach, which was literally right across the street. Did I mention she now lives in a mansion? I laid on the sand and cried loudly, most likely disturbing the high-class Malibu beachgoers. But I didn't care. I'm getting less and less embarrassed about crying in public as time goes on. After all, I've clearly had lots of practice.

All I could think about was how terrible of a failure I was. I felt ridiculous, embarrassed, and impulsive. That puppy needed me, and I let her down.

The next day I went to a dear friend's birthday party. I was still an emotional roller coaster from the canine whiplash the day before. But I showed up, trying to be ready to party.

"Can I bring anything?" I texted.

"Nope! Just yourself!"

"Are you sure?"

"Just you, Jax. Bring yourself."

I showed up to a house full of kind souls, warm food, and not a single job to do. After my failures the day before, part of me showed up needing to earn my purpose back. I needed to prove my worth somehow, whether it was cooking a meal or cleaning a bathroom. I sat down at the kitchen table, again offering to help but being instantly turned down.

"You're sure you don't need anything done?"

"Jackie, please just enjoy yourself," my friend responded after placing a mimosa on the table in front of me.

I sat there watching my friends prepare the rest of the meal. I was literally the only one not doing anything. This was torture. I stared at my mimosa, feeling guilty for not pouring it myself.

"Jax, we're so happy you're here. You're making this house feel like home."

In that moment, surrounded by friends that felt closer than family, without a task to do or a person to help, I finally could breathe. I belonged there. Not because I was helping, not because I was being useful, just because I was me. That was my sanctuary. I wasn't scurrying around completing tasks to prove worthy of my spot at the table. I wasn't volunteering to take the group photos or serve the cake. I was just there. I was probably the least useful person in that house, but in that home, that was okay. I was still loved, I still belonged, and no matter how uncomfortable it made me there was nothing I could do to earn that place at the table.

"I love you guys. Thank you for loving me too."

VI

When I was living in Boston, someone very close to me came out as bisexual. I was sitting down waiting for a train when I found out. I heard her story, broke down in tears, and I didn't know how to explain why. In that train station, I quickly realized that I was about to be involved in a conversation bigger and more telling for who I am as a human being than I could have ever imagined. A conversation that would stretch me in more ways than I was prepared for.

I grew up in a household where people who were meant to be spiritual leaders held up a fake gun to shoot gay characters on TV. That being said, I was well acquainted with the nitty gritty depths of what I was in for. For most of my life, I intentionally avoided the conversation on whether or not homosexuality was right or wrong. The controversy intimidated me. I was well aware of what the popular Christian view on it was, well aware that the majority of the people I was around would say the LGBTQ community is destined for hell. Before now, to avoid the tension, I avoided the whole conversation.

But after this loved one of mine came out, avoiding this conversation was no longer an option. When she came out, I was not only looking at her sexuality in a new way, but I was now exposed to facing my own as well.

Now, I'm about to say something that I never, never ever in one billion trillion years thought I would say out loud, nonetheless write in a book for anyone and everyone to read. Are you ready? I, also, am bisexual. There, I said it.

I have known this to be true about myself since I was twelve years old. I was confused and ashamed and terrified of what it meant for me. And, being bisexual, I was also attracted to men, so I didn't have much of a problem getting away with keeping that other half of myself hidden for so long. But when someone so close to me came out and shared her story ringing so similar to my own, it awakened that part of me that I have tried so long and hard to keep at bay. I realized that my sexuality is a core and primary part of who I am, yet I have shoved it so far out of reach for too long. Back when I was in Boston and she came out, I was nowhere near ready to look inwards at this part of my life. I was so far from a safe place for myself to carry that weight. I wasn't connected to my body in a sacred enough way to do so. I decided to stay hidden.

I loved this person who came out more than I have words for, and I wanted to know how to be there for her. I wanted to know how to have this conversation, how to reconcile that with the evangelical Church world that I had been enveloped in for the past four years. I had work to do.

So, I read book after book, studied passage after passage, and asked a million questions to a million different people. The idea of being both queer and Christian is unfortunately laughable to many people. That breaks my heart, and I wouldn't dare settle there. The conversations that took place around me made it clear that this was something I needed to be prepared to lose friends over. Once I took this stance, things were going to change in my life, and it was going to hurt.

Quickly into doing the work, I realized how easy it was to deconstruct. However, once this part of my faith was pulled apart enough to prove so much of what I had once seen as truth to be flawed, I was horrified. *Why do I believe what I believe?* I'd ask myself.

"Don't ask too many questions, Jackie. You can explain anything away in the Bible if you look hard enough," I was told by different spiritual leaders in my life.

But I didn't listen to them. No one could convince me that my questions were inappropriate, that my wonderings were unnecessary. I realized that if there is a question big enough to explain away God, then whatever god that is, is much too small. I don't have interest in that version. If I'm basing my whole life around something, I need to know why. I need to be allowed to dig a little deeper.

Throughout my days of wondering, journeying through these spiritual questions, reflecting back on the four years I was deep diving into the Evangelical world, I found myself in too many conversations that shattered me. As soon as I started becoming vocal about supporting my loved one, everybody thought it was appropriate to come and tell me what they thought about homosexuality. And I wasn't even out of the closet yet! They did this simply because I had become an ally.

199

"Those people stand for everything that's evil and hateful in the world!"

"You need to pick Jesus or your loved one," people would say, not realizing that their words were also pointed at me.

I had two choices in front of me: I could either jump into the popular side of the conversation, keep my mouth shut, stay in the closet and move along safely, or I could dig a little deeper. I could stand up. I could find out what I believed and why. I could speak up, lose a few people, but gain so much more of who I am. I chose to stand up.

By taking that route, I ended up sacrificing more than I expected. Church didn't feel as safe to me as it used to, and that was something I needed space to grieve. Certain friends I had once held so close suddenly didn't come around anymore. That needed to be grieved as well. Family members, ones that claimed they just wanted me to be happy, considered me stupid, unable to think for myself, and condemned me as well.

Throughout this faith deconstruction I was walking through, I felt as if I was in some sort of wilderness. For a moment, it was desperately lonely. It was isolating not being a part of the groups and communities I once found my identity in. Communities that I used to think I belonged to.

As time passed slowly by, as I reached the other side of what felt like a never-ending panic attack called deconstruction, I started to feel free. A new freedom that I had never felt before. I looked around and discovered that I wasn't alone in this wilderness after all. Somehow in the midst of asking these questions some would consider blasphemy, I stumbled into this beautiful, pure, authentic community of open-minded people as well. I wasn't alone, and I found myself surrounded by people who celebrated the fact that I was, in fact, digging a little deeper. I found my people.

My faith, my spirituality, my views and opinions are *mine*. Those days in ministry school, those overly spiritual friends who stabbed me in the back too many times to count and put God's name on it to make it seem okay, those family "Bible studies" where my dad would slam his fists down to shake the table reading Revelation in order to scare us into heaven, none of that belonged with me. My faith is *mine*. Nobody can take that away from me. Nobody can tell me what I'm supposed to believe, what church I'm supposed to go to, or what laws I need to follow. The more I've deconstructed what I believe to be true and why, the more my eyes have been opened to the real people standing right in front of me. Real people who are different than me, who grew up raised in different households with different cultures and have so much to teach me about life and God.

Finding belonging in a church setting is messy, complicated, and has the potential to sting in ways that I never imagined could hurt so much. Church is a place that claims itself to be home the second you walk in the door. It's filled with people claiming to be family, and a lot of the time that works out beautifully. I still have the most incredibly loving friends involved in these churches, and so deeply love them with all that I have. But what happens when that doesn't remain true? What about the people on the outside, the ones who look different than everyone else? What happens when suddenly your opinions don't match theirs, and they leave you stranded?

On Halloween of 2018, I did what I thought I would never do. I, Jackie Gronlund, came out of the closet. I am both queer and Christian, and I'm learning more of what that looks like every single day. I've learned that on this side of hiding, on this side of fear, there's a lot more room for love. There's a lot more room for human experience, for the freedom to discover just how big God really is. Just how layered and nuanced and complex this world truly is. When I came out, I felt as if I had finally broken out of a tiny little box I was trying to squeeze myself into for my whole life. Our sexuality is such a core part of who we are. I don't want to hide mine. I don't want to ignore it or feel shame when it doesn't look how I thought it was supposed to.

My faith is constantly growing, constantly stretching, and constantly changing. But that's okay! For goodness sakes, if I had all of this faith stuff figured out at nineteen when I first claimed myself as a Christian, I would be living an extremely small, quiet, and scared life. I never want to stop learning more of who God is, and more of who I am alongside of that.

One of my best friends, Amy Pape, told me once that she believes that understanding God is like a big puzzle. Each of us have our own experiences as we go through life. Where we grew up, how we were raised, what churches we were exposed to, what friends we had, each part plays a role in who we become. As we gain these experiences and develop a relationship with who we know God to be, we start to develop our own piece of the puzzle. Sometimes our piece looks different than our friend's or family's pieces. When we meet other people who have different beliefs and have experienced God differently than us, whether that's through their culture or religion or background, we get to see a whole new different piece of a really big puzzle. Some pieces we come across fit neatly next to our own, and some don't. But the more people we meet, the more conversations we have from the humble place of learning rather than condemning, of loving rather than judging, the more pieces of the puzzle we get to see. The clearer picture of God we get to experience. That is how I want to live my life. God bless you, Amy Pape

.

VII

"Jackie, I know we have never met before, but I have watched your videos over the past six or seven months, and I know in my heart that if it's not you, I'm single till I'm thirty."

This was a text message from a boy that I had never met about a been a week after I left Boston. A week since I put my story out on the table, exposed my naked heart and soul and got sent away. In conversations about depression for the first time, anxiety, eating disorders, you name it.

"Jackie," my sister said to me. "I know you don't want to hear this, but I feel like you need to be single for like, at least a year. You've been through a lot, you're working through a lot, and I just don't want you to jump into something before you're emotionally ready."

A few weeks after receiving this text message from a boy I had never met, he was on a plane out to meet and pursue me in Los Angeles. That being said, no, I did not listen to my sister.

I woke up early the morning he would arrive. My hopes were high, and my hair was perfectly curled. This is it. This is my moment. *Maybe he really does love me, maybe he really does have a life to offer me like he claims to,* I thought to myself as I finished my last bit of makeup. Part of this felt like an escape, a new hiding spot from the reality of my own mind, but I ignored it.

Stuck in traffic, as usual in LA, the messages he had sent to me over the past month of getting to know each other crossed my mind. I told him I wasn't okay, told him he had no way of possibly understanding what I had just been through, and how I was scared that I might be jumping into this sooner than I should be.

"I want to come to LA, treat you so freaking well that you cry in awe. The only red flag I see in you is that you don't value yourself enough and I want to help you change that. I want to be your knight in shining armor. I want to be a big neon sign pointing to Jesus for you," were some of the messages he sent that came to my mind.

"This feels weird," I processed out loud alone in my car. "It feels too good to be true. Like a get out of jail free card or something."

I pull up to the airport, and there he was. In person for the first time, I see my "knight in shining armor" eye to eye.

He planned our first date before we met and sent me a necklace with coordinates to the location for Christmas. He wanted us to climb up a mountain and tell each other all of our deepest darkest secrets. In his words, "get all of the skeletons out of the closest."

His plan for romance was underdeveloped, and we couldn't find the coordinates. Turns out they were behind some metal barbed wire fence or something. So, we settled for a different mountain. My stomach started to hurt as we hiked, but I didn't say anything. Something wasn't right, but it has to just be me. *I don't know him, I just met him today, and he wants me to pour out my heart right here right now,* I thought to myself.

We sat down on a rock as the sun started to set, and he decided to go first. He seemed nervous yet oddly confident as he shared his story, as if he had rehearsed it plenty before. I heard him. I heard the skeletons he dug up to share with me, but all I could think of was my own baggage. Baggage I had yet to work through. If he was really as perfect for me as he thought he was, if we're really "destined to be together" like he said we were, why did I feel this scared to tell him my stuff? And why did I have to do it so soon?

It was my turn to share, so I bit my lip and began to open up about my story. I was nervous and unsure where to start, so I talked about dolphins and softball for the first ten minutes before I got to the good stuff. As I shared, I felt like I was sitting in front of a camera, adjusting the lighting as I prepared to make a video to put up on the internet as I generally do. *I have to keep it together*, I thought.

My story ended with a pretty bow tied around the morally acceptable conclusion that brought me there to that mountain, and I felt a huge relief. I was done now. He's still there. I didn't say enough to scare him, but just enough to let him feel like he got what he wanted.

"Okay, Jackie, I'm in. I want to be with you," he said as he pulled me in for our first kiss.

We went back to my apartment and turned on a TV show to end the night. I sat there anxiously remembering the story that I told him earlier on the mountain, making sure I didn't leave anything major out. *Did I forget a guy I had been with? How many details was he actually expecting?*

"I feel like, since I don't have a history with drinking or with sleeping with girls, maybe I can be a part of the redemption to your story," he told me.

He leaned in to kiss me, more aggressively than I anticipated, and things started to heat up. *Was this what he was so excited for, for visiting me in LA?* I felt broken, embarrassed, like I was some project he came to fix. Like my story was taken away from me and instead became a part of his heroism. My story was his now. I was his now. I wasn't even telling him everything, he still didn't know the full depth of pain that I encountered in Boston, but I didn't feel like I wanted him to.

"Jackie, I have to tell you something," he said as he sat up from being on top of me on the couch.

No, I know what you're going to say, don't say it. I thought to myself.

"What?" I asked out loud.

"I could do anything I want to you right now," he started, "but I won't, because I love you."

I sat up, pushed him back a little bit and instantly shut down. *What do you mean you can do anything you want to me? Is that supposed to mean I'm just so easy since I have a past, and you don't? That I would be down for whatever but you're the hero?*

"We'll talk about this tomorrow," I responded.

I went into my room and laid down on my bed. Was I wrong for not saying it back? Did he actually mean that in the way it sounded? It sounded terrible. Does he actually even love me, or is this just the next step he planned out in his plan to *redeem* me? Should I be in this? I just met him. This is way too soon. But how does it make any sense at all to not escape into this relationship?

His time in LA ended four long days later. Our long-distance relationship began to take its natural course of Facetimes, phone calls, and too much texting. I was in and out of counseling sessions regularly but never felt the ability to open up about what was going on with him there. I felt torn, like I was leading two separate lives. One in which I was trying to heal, trying to do the work of mending my soul and processing through traumas in the best way I could. The other part of me felt like it was still hiding, still pretending things were different than they were.

He quickly planned out the rest of our lives, from how many kids we would have to where we would go on our honeymoon. It felt surreal in a very confusing way.

"Hey, can I ask you a question?" I asked as I called my best friend in the world, Amy Pape.

"Of course, Jackie G! Ask me anything."

"What do you think of my boyfriend? Do you like him?"

"Well, do *you* like him? What do *you* think of him? That's what matters," she answered hesitantly. I could tell there was something off, but I lost the ability to communicate that.

"Yeah, he's great!" I answered back enthusiastically, not sure how to express my uneasiness.

Late one night, he called me on the phone to talk. I wasn't really in the mood. I was tired and wanted to go to bed. But as a long-distance girlfriend, I felt like it was my duty to participate.

"Jackie," he told me. "If I move to LA to be with you, it would mean turning my back on all my family, friends, and business."

"Wait, what? To be with me? I thought you said you wanted to move to LA since you were little? Why are you all of a sudden saying you're throwing all of this away for me?"

"Yeah, someday I guess, but of course I'd move there soon for the girl I'm going to marry."

I opened my mouth to respond, but no words came out. I had nothing. My heart started racing and I felt like I was at the end of a cliff, doing everything in my power not to jump off. I was too tired for this.

"Jax, are you okay?"

"I'm fine. I'm just tired. I have to go. I'll text you tomorrow."

"Okay, night, babe. Love you."

The next morning I woke up early, drank two cups of coffee and locked myself in my bathroom to do my makeup. My phone buzzed. It was Megan. She, out of all my friends, is usually the first one to notice when I'm hiding from something hard. Multiple occasions during my time in Boston she tried calling me, and I ignored her. Almost every phone call I dodged, every text message, questions of how I was *really* doing, I didn't answer. It's clear to me today that I was in survival mode in Boston. Hiding was my drug of choice, and vulnerable conversations with someone who *really* knew me, were not an option.

"Hi!" I answered anxiously as I put my phone on speaker so I could continue doing my makeup.

"Hey, how's it going bud?"

"I'm fine."

"You're fine? You don't really sound fine…"

"I'm just stressed."

"Jax, you've been radio silent lately. What's going on?"

I couldn't keep myself together for one second longer. "It's my boyfriend. He's talking about moving here, turning his back on his friends and family and business because he says I'm the girl he's gonna marry. I still feel like I don't even know him! He wants me to fit into his world, but I can't do it. I can't handle this. I don't trust myself to do the right thing here. I'm too impulsive and afraid of commitment and just downright unstable right now! I have too much work to do on myself, I can't just hide in this weird relationship while he pretends to be my hero. And he's already planning his trip to visit next month, and I don't even want him to!"

"Jackie, you don't have to do this. Do you know that?"

"What do you mean I don't have to do this?"

"I mean you literally don't have to do this. You're not stuck. You have only been with this guy for what, three months? You've only spent what, thirteen total days with him in person? You don't have to do this."

"I've gotta go, I'll call you later."

I hung up the phone, ran out of the bathroom, grabbed my sneakers and drove to a mountain. I don't normally climb mountains when I'm upset, but I felt like I couldn't breathe unless I did exactly that, in that exact moment.

One step after the next, I began my excursion up this trail, and let everything out. Being the only one hiking at this moment, it gave me a lot of free-dom to process my life out loud, which I took full advantage of.

"What is wrong with me?!" I yell. "Why am I so scared to make a damn decision? Why do I feel stuck with this guy that I have barely even known for three months? He says he has this big plan, this big dream for our lives, that I just get to be rescued off into his world and out of mine."

In this relationship, I was hiding. I was hiding from myself, my pain, my story, and letting him write it for me instead. He wanted my power, and I handed it over. At the rockiest rock bottom I had been in, the thought of a knight in shining armor coming to rescue me, no matter how *too-good-to-be-true* it felt, I took it. It was my easy button, my ticket out from doing the work of dealing with my mental health on my own. Instead of doing the work, instead of taking charge of my own life and learning how to love the body and soul that I was living inside, I gave him the pen to write my story instead.

I reached the top of the mountain in about an hour, and finally let out my last tear. This hike was a battle, a dramatic one that I now realized I actually was not alone on as I began to be greeted by more hikers coming up behind me that most likely heard every little bit of my dramatic monologue.

I finished the annoyingly necessary small talk with my surprised fellow hikers and found a little-secluded spot by a tree stump to get back to my life crisis.

"I need to break up with him. I can't hide in this relationship anymore. I need to take my power back. Damn it, I make good decisions! I MAKE GOOD DECISIONS!"

Okay, I really needed to stop yelling things to myself in public(ish) places and I knew it, but this was my moment. I didn't trust myself, and I needed that to change. Not only did I need to start trusting the friends around me enough to let them see me in my brokenness, but I needed to trust myself enough to take my own life back. Rather than diving into one impulsive move to the next, I needed to let myself *be*. I needed rest. I needed recovery. I needed *me*.

I am broken, I am depressed, I am exhausted, I am insecure, I am ashamed, but I am *me*. I need *me* back. I need my messiness, I need my cracks and shambles and awkward word stumbling around half sentences I didn't know how to finish. I didn't need someone erasing my hurt and claiming my redemption as their victory. That was the only way I will ever become a whole human again. It's time I take my power back. It's time I find my way back home in my own skin. This is my time. I'm done hiding.

VIII

I have a friend named Amy Pape. Amy has been in my life for about three and a half years now and is someone who I would consider to be one of my best friends. The term *best friend* has left me scarred throughout my life. But Amy Pape has constantly proven the lies that those scars have left wrong. When I feel ugly, she shows me that I'm not. When I feel hopeless, disgusting, unloved, broken, she reminds me who I am.

Tonight was the most magical night that I've had in a very long time. It was spent on a beach sitting beside Amy Pape, amongst a picnic and a sunset. Our menu consisted of sushi, carrots, blueberries, cheese crackers, and chocolate covered almonds. No food group got left behind.

On my drive to pick up Amy, I felt nervous. Life had been wringing my neck lately. I was under the impression that once I left Boston, once I returned to my friends and familiar roads and coffee shops, I would be okay. I thought that if that happened, resilience would take center stage and I would instantly unwrap answers. I hoped and prayed that the relationships that were shattered to pieces at the beginning of this journey would be healed by now, but they weren't. I so badly wanted *that* to be the version of my story that I got to tell Amy Pape.

The words that my counselor spoke to me in our first session echoed in my ears.

"These next choices that you make for your mental health, Jackie, are vital."

Just a week or so ago, five months after this original counseling session, I was meeting with a different therapist who had the same exact conversation with me as the first one did back in January. With even more urgency in her voice than the one before, she proceeded to inform me that I have everyone else fooled, but not her. She can see through my smile and hear through my laughter.

I can't tell you how ashamed with myself I was as I left her office that day. The walk back to my car felt like too far a journey to make alone with how fragile I was, so I called my sister to process it out loud.

"Aren't I supposed to be better by now? How can I possibly be stuck here, still? I thought I was an overcomer. I thought I could persevere through this," I blurted out over the phone. No matter how desperately I wished it wasn't real, the image of my counselor's face smothered in concern was ingrained in my mind.

Depression is an excruciating, isolating, exhausting burden to bear. One minute everything is normal, butterflies are flying and birds are chirping. Then suddenly the downward spiral swallows me right up and the uninvited Darkness arrives once again. Before I know it, there are the voices in my head screaming, "THERE'S NO HOPE. EVERYTHING IS POINTLESS. NOBODY WANTS YOU. YOU MIGHT AS WELL JUST DIE."

Then comes the most dreadful part of all. My mind starts to suggest ideas, circumstances that seemed to offer an escape. "Maybe ending it all, ending your life now would be the easier thing to do," it claimed.

Nothing, absolutely nothing is as agonizing as not finding an end to that. Nothing makes me feel more like a deranged human being than when I'm surrounded by people I love, but my head feels like it's trapped in hell.

I can't help but think, *what if there aren't answers? What if I never find this peace that I keep longing for to call home? Why does it seem as if everyone has the secret to belonging, but nobody is telling me?* It's lonely in here. I need a way out.

If there is truly no way of bypassing suffering, and frankly, we need it in order to experience any sort of an impactful life, maybe home is a place where that tension is welcome. I've been waiting for myself to get to this place of pain-free, all questions answered, tranquil headspace in order to call what I feel home. I'm starting to see that I was wrong. Home is far from the absence of pain.

Belonging, acceptance, and love—those are the primary descriptors of every piece of this quest that I've named finding home. Whether that's through a fresh start in a new city, a prestigious job, above and beyond intellect, perfect body image, whatever. Belonging was what was being sought after all along. Yet even with those all in place, I'd be fooling myself if I believed that I'd find absolute perfection. Even in the most seemingly *perfect* environments, pain is still present. Questions still don't have answers. Heartache will occur, *still*. The relationships that are reminiscent of home are not flawless, nor the city or the job, or the nostalgia brought through the memories of *the good old days*.

As I headed to pick up Amy Pape, these thoughts flooded my mind.

"What if all of this is too much for her, too? What if these broken, messy stories and pieces of who I am are too great a burden to bear after all?"

For too long, I've avoided vulnerability. For too long, I've kept myself hidden. I'm still in pain, I'm still recovering, but who isn't? I'm so damn tired of feeling like my story needs to be hidden until perfect.

Amy Pape embodies love, wisdom, and humility in a way that I've never seen anyone else do. For as long as I've known her, I've witnessed her create so much space for me to learn what it looks like to genuinely be *me*. To learn what it looks like to be human and unlearn what doesn't. Space to process, to wrestle through the nuances that life offers about faith, heartache, and love. She makes space for my doubts and unanswered questions and sits with me in the middle of them. Amy Pape is one of the few people in this world that I have met that creates an atmosphere where it's safe to not know the answer. And when I don't, there has never once been a time when I have been made to feel less than in her presence. That's an environment where growth is inevitable. She isn't the kind of person who will *tell* you she's a safe space, tells you to trust her and to feel okay. Rather, she *shows* you.

When Amy Pape tells me how much she loves me, I believe her. That's a difficult thing to do sometimes, you know? Anyone can speak those words, but a rare few are capable of the actions to show that they're true. The actions and life that follow the words are what proves them as authentic, and not everybody has the ability to offer that. Amy Pape does. She's gonna change the world someday. She already has.

"Hey, Papes," I said cheerfully as she jumped into my car.

"Jackie G! Oh, I just love you so much! I'm so glad to see you! How are you, sweet friend?"

"I'm great!" I answered dishonestly. "How are you?"

I instantly felt guilty. I lied, and to Amy Pape of all people. Why would I do that? When has she ever proven to not be a safe place for me to be honest about where I'm at? I felt like a fraud for telling her I was great when I was so far from it. I was *still* as depressed as I had ever been, and I was tired of listening to the voice that convinced me people would be disappointed in that.

"Amy, I'm not okay."

"Jackie G, I love you. You are making a difference in the world. You matter. Your voice matters. Anything that makes you feel less than any of that is not the truth. I'm here to listen to whatever it is you want to share."

Five months ago when I left Boston, I was drowning under the weight of depression heavier than I had ever been before. I wouldn't have dared to ask anyone for help. I kept the Darkness locked up inside as tight as I could, isolated and safe from anyone to assume otherwise, while I tried to live this carefree happy-go-lucky life on the outside. But as I sat there with Amy Pape, unhealed, unperfect, still learning, patterns must change.

I think the Christian church world has done a bit more damage than not when it comes to our mental health. Not every church or every Christian, by all means; there's layers of both good and bad in every-thing. But one specific way that the church has dis-torted our views on mental health is that somewhere along the lines, we came up with this idea that if we're a Christian, we're supposed to be happy and perfect all the time. If we're truly "saved," we have no problems in life and if we do have problems along the way it's because we don't have enough faith. If we aren't robotically happy, we have become lost sheep needing a savior. I think that's all a bunch of bullshit. Excuse my language.

I don't think God ever once expected us to be perfect. By the church convincing people that they're supposed to be fully joyful at all times, they're shov-ing people farther and farther down the rabbit hole that is isolation, shame, and self-hatred. That is be-cause life is hard. Life is so, damn, hard. We can't sit back and exile other people, much less ourselves, for feeling a little bit of that pain. People work incredibly hard to clean up their outsides, making sure there is a flashy smile followed by an aesthetically pleasing Instagram post to convince the world that they're do-ing wonderful. When the truth is, they're drowning, but unable to ask for help because we've been conditioned to believe that there's shame in that. We've been trained to believe that unhappiness is a shameful lie.

With tears in her eyes, Amy Pape looked at me and said, "Jackie, I feel so loved when you open up and share these parts of your heart with me. Both the good *and* the hard. We're all figuring this out. We all mess up. We learn. And we celebrate both parts because one can't happen without the other. That is your five-month celebration, Jackie G; letting some-one into this with you. That's a massive win."

With tears in my eyes right back, I realized that that was everything my soul needed to hear. It was as if all the blind spots in my rear-view mirror were gone, and suddenly I could see again. Maybe these past five months weren't about me magically getting healed and better. Instead, maybe it was more about me learning that in the process of it all, I'm okay. Perhaps it was about me learning how to invite others into the mess alongside of me, and that I'm not insane for having this story be a chapter in my life. If I let people know what's going on, *maybe they won't leave.*

Friendship has a tendency to lean back in the front seat of our car, checking the blind spots we can't see on our own through the rearview mirror. Amy Pape did this for me on the beach that night.

Home is a place where it's safe to change our minds. It's safe to daydream, wonder, and contemplate the deepest of life's questions. It feels like a heavy awareness of my humanity, and a celebration for that regardless of what it looks like. My humanity is beautiful. My humanity matters. My life matters. And on days when the burden feels like too much to bear, home is knowing that I don't have to carry it alone.

Home is where a mess might be found, but I'm not exiled because of it. It's a place where socks don't always match, and the cereal might get a little soggy. Someone might tape over your favorite episode of Friends, and there are a few peanut butter stains on the couch.

Yet home is where a family gathers. Where you're weak, they're strong. Where they're weak, you're strong, and even when the mistakes happen no one gives up on the other because of them. It's where hiding is unnecessary because even on the bad days, even on the darkest days of all, we're still loved with every ounce of love this universe has to offer.

Love is always growing, always believing, always welcoming and warm. Love shows up, it holds, it hugs, it listens. Love is the most complex, intricate, magical gift we get to embody. Love doesn't just say, ask, or listen. Love acts. Love does. Love includes, not excludes. Love welcomes, not shuts the door. Love invites, it doesn't turn its back. Love is a big room full of big-hearted people who *show up*.

This world is drowning in unanswered questions, flooded in confusion, overwhelmed in tension and nuance. It's a world painted gray, not black and white. A contrast of sorrow in the presence of bliss. What does that mean for us? Where do we go from here? How do we know who to trust so our hearts can remain safe? This journey to discover belonging has brought vibrant beauty to a life that finds resolve in the midst of tension. The perfect picture I was hoping to paint still has smudges, still holds cracks, and the colors don't by any means remain inside the lines. I'm ready to move into a new home where that's what's celebrated. I'm ready to love myself enough to let myself live in a space where that is the norm.

home

It's pouring rain outside. The drops are slapping loudly against my bedroom window as if they've showed up with a vengeance. They have a presence, a voice, and they will not be ignored. I'm packing up the last remnants of the life my LA apartment has housed this year. Tomorrow, I'm moving again, back to Nashville.

I feel embarrassed that I move so much. Some say that it's normal to have so many transitions in your twenties, but they claim that without knowing just how many I've actually had. I appreciate the sentiment, but I would be lying if I didn't say my life is a little out of the ordinary. Within each move that I've made over the past four years, I have claimed it's *the one*. I proudly announce that I've finally found my home, my people, my place in the world, and that "I'm here for good!" Yet here I am, packing up my life yet again.

The truth is, I don't know much more about what direction my life is heading in now than I did at the start of writing this book. Which, honestly, would be a major disappointment to my past self. I'm deeply sorry, Jackie of last year, you haven't reached all the answers and closure you thought you would by now. But on a bit of a blunter note, *no duh*, past Jackie.

One moment I'm under the impression that I'm going to train dolphins on some island in the middle of the Atlantic, the next I think I'm touring the country with rock bands for the rest of my life. Then, out of nowhere, I find myself bemoaning through a Jane Austen novel in the Harvard Library. I get it, I'm impulsive. I have a lot of dreams and passions and it's a rare day that I say the word "no." I mean, I did buy a puppy out of the backseat of a car in an abandoned parking lot. My hastiness is no secret.

My life has taken more than a handful of unanticipated twists and turns, and I'm not going to be surprised if there's a few more waiting down the road. To be honest, I hope there are. I hope I fall down a few more times. I hope I live a life filled with more stories to tell, and more people to learn from. I hope I get my heart broken, and I hope I gain a hell of a lot of wisdom on the other side. And in the middle of it all, I hope I'll remember that I'm still *okay*.

As I stuff my brown boxes tight with the memories this chapter of home LA offered me, I realize that I've never felt more *me*. I'm an incredibly flawed human being. I'm still wrestling with depression, still go days without eating real meals. I still make mistakes, plenty of them. Sometimes I forget to shut the door to my room, resulting in my sister's dog eating six pairs of my underwear almost leading to his deathbed. Thousands of dollars later, he's okay, don't worry. He's back to his same old little asshole self. But I talk about it now. I'm not hiding anymore. I'm letting the entirety of who I am be seen.

As I start to sweep up the dust from underneath my bookshelf, I see a movie stub laying on the floor. I pick it up and instantly remember the date that took me. I remember him reaching to hold my hand. I didn't want him to, but I remember letting him anyway.

I wasn't ready yet. I didn't know how to speak up for myself.

Under the bookshelf is now swept, and I move to clean inside my closet. I kneel down to pick up the scattered pieces of clothing spread out amongst my shoes, and my hand scrapes something sharp.

"What in the world?" I whisper.

I move the clothes to the side and find an old chipped wine glass, still barely scented with the pinot noir it held the night I broke up with a boy I never really liked. This was another guy that claimed we were destiny. He mapped out our future together, speaking boldly about the places we'd travel to and the love we would share. We had only known each other for about a week. Turns out he was wrong after all. Sorry, bro. Looks like you have to find another damsel in distress to make you feel like a hero.

I finish packing up my closet and move into the kitchen. That's where I find my eclectic assortment of mugs. Precious, colorful ones that had followed along through the various moves I had made since I first stepped out of my parent's house at nineteen. Within each move my belongings dwindled down to barely nothing, but those mugs never failed to make the cut. They held the sacred cups of coffee that accompanied me each and every morning next to my journal. I pause before wrapping them up. My hands suddenly feel free, and my heart whole. I sit down on the kitchen floor and take in the sudden life that fills my body. I feel it pour into my fingers, toes, and mind. Out of the abundance of spontaneous, impulsive, nomadic excursions that I had found myself on over the past four years, those loyal mornings never wavered.

I try to hit the bed early, as I plan on leaving for my drive to Nashville at about 4 am. I lay down on my mattress that never quite made it onto a bed frame, stare at the empty walls that I never found the pictures to cover and breathe in deep. Was this apartment ever really my *home*?

4 am comes quick and I roll over to turn my alarm off before it wakes up my roommate. I throw water on my face, grab my last few bags and walk out to my car. I turn on the song I always start my road trips with: *Uncharted* by the one and only Sara Bareilles. She is a queen, and I'm taking this moment to make that known. I turn onto the freeway and make my way east.

"I think I'm on my way home now," I whisper.

There's fifteen hours in front of me for the first leg of this road trip. I've never driven that far by myself. But as I watch the sun peek out from beneath the ground, I realize how therapeutic this drive is about to be.

I have a history with not doing great for extended amounts of times alone. I tend to think too much and get swallowed up by my own anxiety. I swear I get alone for five minutes too long and I become fully convinced that nobody loves me, cares about me, and that I'm all alone in the world. But this morning, watching the magic in the sunrise through my windshield, I know that's not true. I know that I am okay.

When I started writing this book, I had no idea how it was going to end. I've been in so many conversations about what the concept of home means and have been given every answer in the world. To some, home is simply a house with a front porch wrapped neatly inside of a white picket fence. To others, home is a person, a pet, a job, or a religion. Sometimes the journey to discover home is spiritual, focused on learning who the Divine really is, and what that means for why we're all here. To others, finding their home looks like finding their person, then building a life worth living together and finding purpose in that. But even in these conversations, I'm still left with the unquenchable answer to my

FINDING HOME

question. What does home mean for *me*? I don't think
I'm going to find that through another person's journey.

When I began this project, I fully expected to
find my answer. I expected it to fit perfectly into a
conclusion for this book and offer people a formulaic
answer to a question I believe the majority of us ponder at some point in our lives. We all have our own
unique answers, and none of them are wrong. None
of our experiences are invalid. Home is not quite as
simple as I once imagined it to be. The journey I've
been on, however, has become more of a journey of
learning who I am. A voyage to step back inside my
own body.

"Who is Jackie?" I ask out loud in my car.
"What does Jackie believe?"

When I'm not relying on someone else to tell
me who I am, what I should do with my life, what I
should and should not believe, the answers to those
questions become a bit more difficult to come by.
Simultaneously, they transform into what's *real*.

"Real is what I want."

What are the answers to those questions, you
ask? I don't know. I wish I did, but I'm okay with not
knowing. I wouldn't have always been okay without

a clear-cut response, but on this road trip today, I am. Maybe it has something to do with the open road, the perfect playlist serenading my every mood, or the wonder in the mountains peeking in through each window of my car.

Whether or not I am drunk on the adventure of this trip, my mind feels just about the clearest it's ever felt right here inside this moment. I feel as if I've been traveling, couch surfing, dragging suitcases through airport terminals, sleeping in busses, hotel rooms, Airbnb's, all looking for this *magic*. Magic that looks like home.

Am I worthy?
Do I belong?
Am I wanted?
Where do I go next?
What is my purpose?
Am I loved?

I chase, I beg, I plead for belonging. I fail, then I leave. When I can't find the perfection I'm looking for to let myself breath, I run away to look elsewhere. I look in careers, intellect, body image, usefulness, spirituality. Then when I fail again, when I don't find that belonging, I hide. I cover up my shortcomings with a sparkly smile and charismatic personality. *If people don't know that I'm dying inside, if they don't get me vulnerable, I'll survive.* Maybe, just maybe, I can find my home there.

I was wrong.

Without the dark, the light wouldn't be light. Light would just be normal. Without rain, the sun wouldn't feel as warm. Without the cracks, the real light would have no room to shine through. I need to stop pretending that pain doesn't exist, and instead open my eyes to the vibrant beauty that it can paint in a story. Beauty that makes a story come to life.

Perhaps that's a little bit more of what home looks like. It's where I'm aware and present to pain and heartache, yet I'm still okay. I choose to show up, *still*. Maybe it's not this picture-perfect white picket fence mentality where I walk inside to freshly baked cookies every day like in The Brady Bunch. Instead, it could be a place where someone might spill the cereal, and that's okay. I think knowing that I'm loved within the chaos says a lot more than pretending it doesn't exist.

It appears to be undeniable that the home I'm searching for is one that is first and foremost carried within my own body. A body that I have fought long and hard to love. A body that I used to dread looking at in the mirror. A body that I have been taught to change, manipulate, and feel ashamed of. I belong here, to me, inside my own skin. I will fight to protect the sanctity of that.

I don't suppose I had to leave Boston in order to reach that conclusion. Frankly, I don't think it matters in the slightest bit what city I'm in or what apartment I move to next. It doesn't matter how many times I move, what my body looks like, what career I have, or what exciting adventure I'm heading on. This voyage I've been on to find home has become one to find *myself*. To truly, deeply, *love* myself. Part of why I felt so far from home in Boston was because I was quickly losing who I was when I was there. I rapidly lost sight of my own passions, my own dreams, favorite meals, sacrificing it all to mold myself into someone else. Shaping myself to fit the mask of someone who I thought would be worthy. Someone that didn't belong to me. I was living inside a body that was not my home.

Finding Home has been a pilgrimage of learning to be okay when I feel ugly. It's a been a quest of learning to look at myself in the mirror and not hate the reflection staring back. It's one where I grow to believe a friend like Amy Pape, telling me I'm beautiful and worthy when my head tells me I'm not. It's one where I continue learning to trust myself and embrace the convictions that are encountered along the way. *Who is Jackie? What does Jackie love? What is Jackie created for?* I think an eating disorder and depression are mere symptoms of neglecting what these questions have been asking.

I know what it feels like to keep my mouth shut when people are saying things that I disagree with. I know what it feels like to blend in and go with the flow out of fear of confrontation. I know what it feels like to not have my own opinion, but to grab hold of someone else's instead. But now, now I know what it feels like to think for myself. Now I know what it feels like to hold power in my voice, my eyes, my being. What would I believe and how I would think if there were no other voices in my head? What does it look like to not need the world's approval of what I look like or how I feel? I think this is it. As I write these words, I feel as if I've uncovered a secret that I've been carrying all along but haven't realized till right now.

I am okay.

Whether I'm depressed, whether I haven't eaten a meal in two weeks, whether I love where I live or have moved twenty times in one year, I am okay. I'm not moving backward, I'm not remaining stagnant, and I'm not going to arrive at a place of perfection no matter how hard I try, or how deceitfully I pretend to. We can't make-believe the pain doesn't exist anymore than we can pretend not to be human. We can't pretend to not have questions any more than we can pretend to have all the answers.

I want to love all of myself. I want to love my cracks, my mistakes, my journey. Even on the days when I feel like the walls are caving in, I am still safe, and my body is still home. I am both beautifully imperfect, and beautifully loved. They are inseparable. That's the secret.

When I left Boston, my mind and body were my own archenemy. I was afraid of what my messiness would do to people. I was scared I was too broken. I embarked on this never-ending adventure of one room to the next, one city to another, looking for an environment that would take all of that pain away.

We're allowed to be an inconvenience. We're allowed to have questions, doubt, uncertainty. We're allowed to be messy. The tattered pieces to our stories are accepted even before they're resolved. We need to remember that.

All this time I have been running from myself, not knowing that *I* was who I needed all along. It's when I'm at peace in my own skin that I am a good friend. It's when I've forgiven myself for where I've messed up that I can offer that same grace to others. It's when I allow myself to be loved that I can then love others. I can then accept others. I can then help other people find home in their bodies as well.

No matter what religion you're subscribed to or faith you hold in your heart, this life will throw chaos your way. Invincibility has never been an option. There will always be pain, brokenness, emptiness, and fear. That's not going anywhere. We can all believe whatever we want will happen after this life passes onto the next. But right here, right now, life is hard.

Glennon Doyle says, "Life is hard—not because we're doing it wrong, just because it's hard." But that doesn't mean that we give up. That doesn't mean that we throw in the towel and hide away behind our smiles or inside our glasses of champagne pretending that the painful reality of the outside world doesn't exist. I did that for far too long, in multiple facets in my life. Once we know what's true, there's no going back to the days when we were ignorant. I can't pretend depression isn't real. It's a hard truth, but the truth is what we want. Getting there, getting to the other side, it's a bumpy road. Rediscovering that bold, unapologetic persona inside that little pink nightgown that I wore as a little four-year-old girl freely dancing around in circles takes work. It takes hard conversations. It takes looking at pieces of life that are inextricably uncomfortable, and sometimes the other side is too far out of reach to be seen. It's still there. The mask is so tempting. It's a quick fix, but it's a lie. The band-aids don't work, and that is what I realized when I hit my breaking point in Boston.

These little whispers of home that I've collected have been remarkably healing for my soul. The conversations where my bare-naked heart is out there in the open with words and sentences all stumbled and clumsy, yet I'm responded to with the deepest sincerity. Being stopped mid-sentence in the middle of a walk down a fall swept road so that my friend's eyes could meet mine as she told me that I mattered. It's the feeling of holding the tears far back into my chest, then being pulled into my sister's arms with the freedom to let them all out. Those are the moments when the mask begins to fall off. The mask has no place in that world. The moments when I'm not pretending, I'm not sending in a seemingly "happier" version of myself to do life in place for me. Instead, I'm taking ownership of my life as *me*. I'm taking my power back. That's home. That's where the longing meets its match.

We need to remind each other how we were meant to live, and what we were meant to feel like. We need to embrace the reality of what it truly means to be *free*. This is where we live right now. These people in our lives are there with a purpose.

This world belongs to us. Somewhere along the lines, it was stolen by a Darkness that does not deserve a place here, nor does it deserve one inside our bodies. We are our strongest allies, we are our only hope of finding this place of sanctuary. It's time to come out of hiding, to put on the only real armor we have and take it back and make it our home once again.

When I was that little girl prancing around my basement in my pink nightgown, I felt at peace with my life because I was okay with being me. Nobody had told me yet that I was imperfect. Nobody had told me that I wasn't pretty enough, smart enough, or skinny enough yet. Then, without asking or being prepared for its arrival, life happened. Darkness showed up. Pain, trauma, depression, eating disorders, toxic relationships, anxiety, they all made their grand appearance. I ran away from these realities that my life had become, looking for every loophole possible. I tried to hold tightly to that innocent little girl but sacrificed reality to do so. If I have learned anything over the past five years since I first started looking inward, it's that there is no growth or life outside of pain.

Life is hard, dammit, and it might feel this way for a while. If I truly want to get back to the genuine peace inside of that little girl's heart, it's not going to look like erasing all of the life that has happened since. It looks like work, hard work, and showing up. It looks like paying attention, being present, and being okay when there's more tension than resolution.

Glennon Doyle says this more perfectly than I'll ever be able to, so I'll write her words here to sum this up: "Life is brutal. But it's also beautiful. Brutiful, I call it. Life's brutal and beautiful are woven together so tightly that they can't be separated. Reject the brutal, reject the beauty."

I look out my rearview mirror to see the sun starting to set behind me. I've been driving for a long time now, and my racing thoughts have made me sleepy. But boy, it feels good.

Never once have I felt more inside my own body. Never, not once, have I ever been as a part of my own humanity as I feel in this moment. In my car, in the middle of the desert, not sure where I am landing or what is happening next, I belong. I belong in my own skin. I belong in my own soul. I belong to myself. I have my power back.

When I stepped off of that plane from Boston back to Nashville, there was a deep intuition in my soul that felt like I had stepped back into my own shoes. It didn't make any sense to me, because I had never felt farther away from myself. I had never felt as broken as I did in that airport leaving Boston. Today, driving in my car, turning another chapter, I understand what my soul was saying. As I stepped off that airplane, I was stepping back into union with who I was all along.

I wasn't hiding. I was *me* again.

"I'm home," I whisper. "A different kind of home."

acknowledgments

Thank you, Amy Pape, for believing in me so deeply, loving me so well, and making space for me to process through both the pain and the excitement that life has thrown around. Thank you for telling me how much I matter when I send you poop emoji texts on the dark days. You've taught me more about unconditional love, friendship and God than I could have ever dreamed of.

Thank you, Lauren, for being such a refreshing bundle of light and joy in a world where it can be hard to find. You always remind me of who I am, and the truth of how much goodness life has to offer. You've cheered me on harder than I could ever deserve.

Thank you, Megan, for being such a constant reminder of how loved I am. Thank you for never giving up on me, and for loving me so well when I didn't know I needed it. Thank you for being honest with me back in September when I was first planning on publishing that other version of this book and encouraging me to be patient with myself. Thank you for listening to whatever nudge you had to write me that letter, and for being such an incredible friend ever since.

Thank you, Alex, for being the best big sister that a girl could ask for. We've had the craziest and weirdest sister relationship in the whole world, and I am so thankful and proud to have you in my life. Thank you for, no matter what is going on between us, to never fail to drop everything and be there for me when I need you. Thank you for fighting for me when I didn't even know how to fight for myself. I've learned more about grace from you than I could ever write in a book. Thank you for teaching me all about clothes, Disney Channel, Hairspray, Everlane, and how to curl my hair with a straightener. Thank you for caring about how I'm doing, calling to check in on me, and not letting me avoid things that are hard. You're incredible at what you do, and I couldn't have written this book without you. Also thank you for letting me use your music for my video, and for helping me design the cover of this book. You rock, don't ever change, have a great summer.

Thank you, Uncle Mike, for being the coolest uncle of all time and pushing me to work hard, dream

big, and not give up. Thank you for all of the opportunities that you've given me over the years for all of
the different career paths I've ventured on to. From
dolphins, to film, to speaking, you've been such an
encouragement through it all. Thank you for what
you do at RYLA and for letting me be a part of it,
and for coming to shoot my book promo video in LA
that one time when it was really hot outside. You,
Mandy, Brealyn, and Tatum mean the absolute world
to me and I'm so happy you're my family.

Thank you, Jess, for being such a light in my
life. It's been an honor to get to do life with you and
your family so closely. Thank you for encouraging
me, teaching me important grocery store routines and
bargain hunting skills, and believing in me so much.
Thank you for letting me lay on your couch on the
dark days and going on adventures with me on the
good ones. I miss you.

Thank you, Sydney and Sehler, for continuing to be such a special part of my life. You two mean
the world to me and I can't wait for us to be partying
in our old people wheelchairs someday. I always
look forward to coming home to see you two, so
thank you for being my friends.

Thank you, Juan, Uncle Mike, Brealyn, Summer, Julia, Megan, and Jess for spending the day helping me create my first book trailer video. It meant so much to me and I'm extremely honored to have you be a part of this project.

Thank you, Trinity, Mrs. Feller, Maddi, and Chris, for helping me edit and proof read my book a million times. You have no idea how much I appreciate the time and energy each of you spent helping me complete this project.

Thank you, Sara Schandelmayer, for being so generous with your talents and time by helping me with the design of the front cover. You are incredible and I am so thankful to have someone like you in my life. So many more Tin Roof nights to come!

Thank you to my Patreon family: Alex G Fan Club, Alex L, Annicka C, Anthony Geoge Kibildis, AnzhelikaB, Austin and Andrew Fathman, Bob Taylor, Carissa Embry, Chris Snuffer, Christopher Soriano, COFFEE_WAVES, Cristian Summerville, Danielle Schuyler, Derek Cavender, Elaine Shaw, Eli Freestone, Emily Crawford, Emily Koth, Erica Dean, Esther E, Ethan Wilson-Bruce, Felicity Townsend, Felicity Townsend, Gerald Perez, Gloria Flores, Hannah Joy Thompson, Hope Davis, Isiah

Harvey, James Nelson Ethridge II, Jen Buckeridge, Joshua Freeman, Julie Knabenshue, Kathryn Eads, Kiersten, Lacey Melin, Larry Lee Lyons Jr, Laura Whitney, Lisa Tempel, matt wright, Meg Roberts, Megan Day, Mia Isaac, Michele Muñoz, Mike L, Miri, MJ, Quas0r, Robert Webber, Sarah Poiesz, Steven Reyes, Sue Basile, Tiffany Ogles, and Torie Horton. Each one of you has changed my life in more ways than I'll ever be able to explain. I wouldn't be able to do any of this without you, so thank you for believing in me and supporting me in all that I do. You guys are the real world-changers here.

Thank you to all the couches that I've slept on, Lyft drivers that picked me up, hotel lobby concierges, Airbnb hosts, and flight attendants that crossed paths with me on my journey to find my home. You made it a whole lot easier, and a whole lot less lonely.

Thank you so much to Falcon Coffee for getting me drunk on Irish Coffee while I pulled my hair out and danced around in circles trying to format this book. Barista Nate, you're the man. Thanks for the whip cream.

Thank you for reading my book, for putting life, purpose, and meaning behind the words that I have written. This whole thing wouldn't have been possible without each and every one of you. I hope my journey finding home has helped you in yours along the way.

FINDING

home

Elise!
You are so kind. Thank
you for wanting to read
my book! ♡ Jackie G